Hit the Bullseye

Hit the Bullseye
How Denominations Can Aim Congregations at the Mission Field

Paul D. Borden

Abingdon Press
Nashville

The Convergence eBook Series

Edited by Tom Bandy and Bill Easum
Copyright © 2003 by Paul D. Borden.
All rights reserved.

This book is printed on acid-free, recycled, elemental-chlorine-free paper.

Library of Congress Cataloging-in-Publication Data

Borden, Paul D.
  Hit the bullseye : how denominations can aim congregations
at the mission field / Paul D. Borden.
      p. cm.—(The convergence ebook series)
  ISBN 0-687-04371-9 (pbk.)
  1. Church renewal. 2. Christian leadership. I. Title. II. Series:
Convergence series.
  BV600.3.B67 2003
  262'.001'7—dc22

                                                        2003019170

Scripture quotations, unless otherwise noted, are from the New Revised Standard Version of the Bible, copyright © 1989, by the Division of Christian Education of the National Council of the Churches of Christ in the United States of America. Used by permission.

04 05 06 07 08 09 10 11-10 9 8 7 6 5 4 3 2

Contents

108847

TO TERESA
You are my muse, my friend, my lover!

It is one experience to think outside the box, it is an entirely different experience to live outside the box. Hit the Bullseye is clearly "outside the box" living. It is a must read for all judicatory and congregational leaders.

—Sam Brink, Minister of Church Resources,
American Baptist Churches of Wisconsin

* *

By focusing congregational support systems on faithfulness to Christ, disciplined commitment to change, and intentional strategies for congregational renewal, Paul Borden and his colleagues in northern California have given mainline Churches a great gift—a visionary action plan of new hope and possibility for churches incapacitated by inertia.

—Ezra Earl Jones, Former General Secretary,
United Methodist Board of Discipleship

* *

Paul Borden is right on the mark in his new book about local church renewal through denominational leaders and judicatories with a focus on the right stuff for the 21st century mainline. He has brought together a powerful emphasis on leadership, mission, vision and core values that actually works. His insight on encouraging and protecting the risk takers is alone worth the price of the book.

This is a must read for every Bishop, District Superintendent, Judicatory Leader, and pastor who is serious about the renewal of the mainline church.

—Dale R. Turner, Norwalk District Superintendent,
East Ohio Conference of The United Methodist Church

* *

Paul offers us, a tried and true road map that clearly delineates landmarks and landmines in the journey of transforming churches, judicatories and conventions from shepherding services to relevant mission outposts. Truly a gift of practical, candid, courageous, clear, challenging and powerful words for today's judicatory, conventions and local church leaders.

—Edward H. Hammett,
Senior Leadership Consultant & Congregational Coach for
Baptist State Convention of North Carolina

Series Foreword

Tom Bandy

Paul Borden's story of the transformation of a middle judicatory is a landmark in the field of church growth. There has been much talk about the disappearance of the "top-down" denominational world, and the emergence of the "bottom-up" independent congregational world, but Paul reveals a third shift. He signals the rise of the "middle-support" world. Transformed congregations can transform denominations if the network grows fast enough. Paul demonstrates that a transformed regional, middle judicatory can transform a multitude of congregations if the leaders change radically enough. The power of middle judicatory support of congregational mission can even ricochet to have impact upon national denominational structures.

The church as a body of Christ is about mission to all peoples, not institutional survival or even care for the membership, and the congregation is the primary unit of that expanding mission. What happens when a denominational middle judicatory takes these simple principles to heart? What happens when judicatory leaders align themselves and every aspect of their organization behind these principles? What happens when it deploys staff, selects and equips pastors, structures decision-making, distributes assets, networks volunteers, and undertakes strategic planning with these principles guiding the budget?

Everywhere I look denominational bodies are trimming budgets, downsizing staff, reducing programs, and retreating to the presumed "core" of activity involving personnel oversight, property management, and public policy pronouncements. Congregations either languish for lack of mission direction, resources, or skills . . . or drift away to find other partners who can help them more effectively. This is the story of a judicatory that dared to travel another path. What Paul has learned about realigning the work of the judicatory can instruct any denominational body struggling to redefine its place in God's postmodern mission.

Foreword

Leith Anderson

> "Some look at things that are, and ask why. I dream of things that never were and ask why not?"
>
> —George Bernard Shaw

There are approximately 400,000 churches in the United States and the vast majority of them belong to denominations. Some are healthy, vibrant, and growing. Most are tired, struggling, not growing, and don't know what to do.

Plenty of critics and cynics take surveys, analyze data, and write books about what is wrong with the churches of America. As if following the theology of Chicken Little they are convinced that the sky is falling and there is little we can do except seek cover. Proposals for renewal often are offered by theorists who tell practitioners what to do but have never actually done it themselves.

What if?

What if there was a way to help declining churches to grow? What if we could teach pastors how to lead their congregations to spiritual renewal? What if thousands of churches changed from maintenance to mission? What if a movement began with 200 churches that grew to 200,000 churches? What if millions of unchurched people came into lasting relationships with Jesus Christ and the church? What if the denominations of America with all of their people, property, and potential became the epicenter of this spiritual earthquake that became known as the Great Awakening of the 21st Century?

Maybe all this sounds too good to be true. Well, it has already begun. Centered in the earthquake zone of northern California, the American Baptist Churches of the West have demonstrated that a plateaued and declining region of mainline congregations can become a model of healthy and growing congregations. They have overcome the usual excuses that "our churches are too small," "we have too many older people and congregations," and "property here is too expensive." They followed a powerful formula of biblical strategies, courageous leadership, and much hard work. What is most amazing is that the turnaround took less than five years.

Why not?

Here is the dream. Denominational leaders, executive ministers, bishops, district superintendents, regional directors, seminary teachers, pastors, and lay leaders will discover what God has done in northern California and say, "Why not here?" With a few creative adaptations we can do the same thing in our denomination and in our churches.

They will start small and multiply. They will risk their traditions, finances, staff, and jobs. They will respond to misunderstanding with teaching and take criticism with grace. Then there will be one successful church transformation—new vision, new faith, new people, and new excitement. One will become ten and ten will become one hundred. Church by church, region by region, denomination by denomination—a true reformation will bring a great new era to the people and churches of our generation. It can be done. It has been done. This is a dream of the way things can be. Be among those who say, "Why not? Let's do it!"

Chapter One
Finding the Right Target
and Hitting It

We live in a time when many people say there is little hope for mainline Protestant denominations. The evidence seems to indicate that such predictions are correct. As congregations, memberships, attendance, and mission dollars decline in relation to former levels, a lack of hope and low morale constrains leaders in many denominations.

One significant part of denominational life is the role that is played by entities called *middle judicatories*. This book offers hope to judicatories and the congregations that comprise them. It suggests the means of transformation and growth for judicatories and congregations. The book will not suggest how national denominational entities can correct their circumstances, but it will demonstrate how judicatories and congregations can again become effective agents of mission. While recognizing various polities involved in different denominational entities, which affect the way judicatories conduct their ministries, I believe the problems they encounter today are common ones that relate more to leadership and changing ministry paradigms. Judicatories and congregations are facing—and in a sense creating—the broader problems that are experienced by entire denominations. If denominations have any hope for the future, it may appear as individual congregations, and in turn middle judicatories, are energized for mission. In this book I intend to offer principles, strategies, and tactics that enabled our judicatory to move from a desire to survive to the evidence of hope, through transformation and growth.

Foundational principles are truths that are transferable across all middle judicatories regardless of polity because they relate to such underlying concepts as mission, vision, values, and structure. Such principles affect the very fabric of both our denominational and institutional identities. Principles relating to leadership, organizational structure and behavior, culture, and how humans behave individually and in groups are as true as those truths upon which we build our theology. The foundational principles in this book are true regardless of how they might be expressed through polities different from my own. I also believe that one reason our judicatories are facing difficult times is because we have either ignored or missed how such principles have impact upon the way we minister and lead our judicatories and congregations.

Strategies are the broad ministry initiatives that judicatories take to accomplish their tasks, such as long-range planning, leadership training, establishing financial priorities, and so forth. Such strategies come out of beliefs about foundational principles in one's polity. If the alignment between foundational principles and strategy is inconsistent, ministry initiatives will fail. Tactics are the specific programs that are designed to accomplish the strategies, such as particular curricula, clergy deployment, and denominational staff development. The goal is clear alignment between the tactics, strategies, and foundational principles.

While foundational principles are transferable across judicatories and congregations, strategies and tactics on the other hand are always influenced by the context in which they are implemented. Therefore in some cases they must be adapted while in other situations some may be ignored and replaced by new ones that fit that context. For example, missionaries have learned that the foundational principles behind their message, call, and character will never change. However, strategies and tactics that work with one group may be quite ineffective with another. Missionaries also realize that strategies and tactics must always be consistent with their principles, while constantly changing in light of culture, as long as such changes do not violate the foundational principles. Finally missionaries have learned that confusion of principles and strategies leads to ineffectiveness and legalism, and then irrelevancy.

As a context for the principles and strategies in this book, we make one basic assumption with two implications. We assume that people leading middle judicatories must believe that the local congregation is the basic unit of mission in the world. Of course, denominational and judicatory leaders affirm this belief often, yet the tragedy is that most have a wide gap between the presumed belief and their daily tasks. Sometimes this belief is more intellectual than foundational. More often, however, this belief is not lived out because traditional and institutional demands make it impossible. For example, prior to reversing the decline in our region I consistently heard pastors tell me that their perception of their role was to lead congregations to financially support the agendas set by national denominational agencies which had been communicated to them through middle judicatory leaders. To the contrary, the core belief about focus on the congregation must inform the behaviors of all judicatory and denominational personnel.

This assumption creates two behavioral changes. The first behavior is a corporate one; the second is more personal. The corporate behavior means that a judicatory intentionally decides to expend the majority of its financial, time, and human resources on meeting congregational needs rather than fulfilling institutional and denominational demands. This requires a conscious decision, in most cases, to literally change how the judicatory functions. It also means that a number of current activities will be abandoned. This abandonment will generate criticism from either people within the judicatory or individuals in national positions. The judicatory must be willing to withstand this conflict and push ahead in focusing on local congregations. The personal behavior refers to perception of judicatory personnel as competent enough to offer congregations substantial aid in helping them grow, or coaching them to move from dysfunction to health if growth is not occurring. Given the obvious scarcity of resources and competition for dollars, it also may mean that some dollars that have normally come to the denomination may need to stay with the congregation for it to have the resources to grow.

In addition to these two behavioral changes, as stated previously two major implications derive from the assumption that the congregation must be treated as the major unit of mission in reaching the world. First, in a day of congregational decline the primary role of judicatories is to be a catalyst for congregational transformation. Second, once a majority of congregations have moved from organizational dysfunction to organizational health, the judicatory's primary role is to be a catalyst for healthy congregations to plant new reproducing congregations. The purpose of focusing on health and growth is to see reproduction occur. Not all growing congregations are healthy ones. However, all *healthy congregations* are growing. They grow by making new disciples for Jesus Christ and they grow by creating new congregations that grow and then reproduce. A judicatory is doing its job well when it is seeing both transformation and reproduction happen regularly and consistently in a majority of its congregations.

Anyone intimately involved with denominational life knows that these implications are not the norm for judicatories. Many leaders today find the very existence and survival of their judicatory to be at stake. There is far more time and effort in keeping the institution going than in focusing resources on the local congregation as the major unit of mission. Change is needed if there is to be hope. And such change is not incremental; it must be systemic for such hope to be realized. This book is an attempt to discuss the systemic changes that are needed. Our story offers hope that fundamental change can occur.

Key Changes for Your Judicatory

We must first develop a new measure of what it means to be successful as a judicatory. We must understand that survival is not success. Neither is merely being a little ahead of last year or being better than a rival judicatory that may at one time have been more successful than ours. I am not defining success as we might in the consumer or business worlds. I am pursuing success in the sense of what we measure, with questions about whether we have accurate ways of measuring our strategies and performance. We recall this definition from the New Testament epistles that are essentially consultations with local congregations about things they had done well or aspects of ministry where they had performed poorly. The apostles evaluated these congregations by a variety of standards. For example, sometimes the Apostle Paul said you are doing it differently than I did when I was with you. On another occasion he said even those outside the church do not do what you are doing. There was the expectation that congregations would measure up and be evaluated. The Revelation of John is very specific about what God wants seven types of congregation to do or stop doing (Revelation 2-3). To see change in congregations and how judicatories relate to congregations, determine what to measure and then evaluate whether we are doing the job effectively or ineffectively. Take seriously the concept of success, as a result to be measured.

The key ingredient needed for change is leadership. Rather than persons appointed by a bureaucracy into leadership positions, I am describing persons who are leaders because people are following them and as a result positive systemic change is occurring. We have observed that the biggest human factor in the process of transforming a dysfunctional congregation to a healthy one is the leadership ability of the pastor. This factor is also characteristic with church planters. The most effective plants are ones with the most effective leaders. For example, a good rider can help a mediocre racehorse win, while a mediocre rider will often cause a good horse to lose. Therefore we are constantly looking for good riders. This also means that we need to rethink what it takes to be a leader in a judicatory. It means looking at individuals who have the gift of leadership or have leadership talents and skills that can be developed and honed. We should think differently about what kind of education, experience, and perspectives are needed to be not only a leader but an agent of change and transformation. Judicatories need courageous risk takers who are women and men of vision, who think missionally, and who can articulate and implement strategies for effective and systemic change. It means finding good leaders who have the courage to perform, the wisdom to know what principles need to be adopted and the insight to implement effective strategies.

Judicatories need to be known for empowering pastors and lay leaders to become agents of change and transformation within their local congregations. This means helping and protecting those leaders and the congregations that are willing to take risks and be different. It means learning how to train, coach, and mentor leaders.

It means functioning in the roles of broker and networker. It means learning to treat each congregation as a micro-culture that must deal with transformation and health in its own unique context.

This book will help you redesign and rethink what is required to make and deploy strong pastoral leaders. Too often in many denominations a seminary degree and ordination are simply union cards guaranteeing someone a position and the title of leader. Yet too often those in positions of leadership are not leaders, do not know how to be effective in ministry, and have little or no idea what their mission is or if they even have one. Many times in life the best leaders are those who were viewed as mavericks while maturing. These people rejected the status quo of life and with insufficient wisdom rebelled. However, with maturity they are often able to channel their dissatisfaction with the mentality of "we have always done it that way before" and take the risks needed to lead productive and effective change. Yet such people in the religious world are often seen as liabilities and therefore create their own parachurch organizations or take on ministries that seem to be apparently hopeless and make them work. We learned that a positive or negative seminary track record often has no correlation to effective leadership. Which is why we should select people in ministry based upon their overall experience rather than what we think their potential might be. Also, success in the academy may reflect gifts and talents that are the opposite of those needed for effective leadership. Scholarship is hard work and often demands people who can work alone and lead themselves, while finding it difficult to lead communities of people on missional and visionary pilgrimages. Too often we base our evaluation for potential leaders upon incorrect assumptions.

None of the changes I see as fundamental will occur without changes in structure. In some denominations this is harder to do than in others since in some cases the denominational connections are so tied to the granting of positions, property, recognition etc. that change is difficult. However, in such cases there may be the need to create shadow structures that are usable and effective, even if they are not recognized officially. However, in all denominations the thought of systemic structural change is so repugnant that it usually does not happen. This is often why a new vision and mission are never implemented, because those who do not like them resist by manipulating current structures that do not fit either the vision or mission. It is at this point that leaders need to step up and take big risks and say the old way is killing us, let's breathe new air, redesign structure, and accomplish the mission.

Most judicatories at this point in time are institutionally driven. Change for such judicatories means becoming missionally driven. However, this change will not occur until there is a different way of thinking about functions that judicatories are called upon to perform. Currently most judicatories have denominational, fiscal, and ceremonial responsibilities along with important social and missionary agendas that occupy much of their energy and time. Added to these concerns often are the oversight of property and other related ministry organizations. And many judicatory officials spend an astonishing amount of time with legal problems pertaining to the pastors and people in their jurisdiction. In fact it is often the pressure of dealing with all these issues, collectively and individually, that cause many judicatories to lose sight of the congregations they are called to serve. Or perhaps it is dealing with these issues and resulting pressures, in the name of congregational service, that prohibit judicatories from being the catalysts for transformation and church planting they should be. Therefore, ways of thinking and functioning are challenged here in order to move from serving institutional needs to leading a mission of change and redemption, without sacrificing the oversight of the institutional.

Finally, for leaders with many years of experience who feel constrained or distant from the systems that they oversee, the changes recommended here presume specific ways of believing and thinking. Some will question the extreme behaviors proposed in this book, so briefly I describe specific theological issues that have shaped our thoughts and in turn our behaviors. Our beliefs about God, Jesus Christ and God's Church may need to change if we are to see our congregations change. If we were to argue backward from behavior to belief as we observe what is happening in judicatories and congregations across North America we would have a very small view of God and God's ability to work. It would seem as though God is weak, finite, and perhaps even incompetent. Or at the very worst God has selected the wrong people to carry out a plan. Apparently God's weakness is revealed through weakness as we look at the Church, which is the opposite of what the Apostle Paul states in Corinthians.

Two Metaphors that Hinder Change

We hear much about paradigms and their influence upon the way we think and in turn behave. Paradigms are simply a way to look at reality. For example a road map is a paradigm. A map provides a way to understand how to navigate a city, state, or nation. We recognize that the lines on the map are representations of roads, streets, and freeways. These representations however, are not actual thoroughfares. Often the mental maps we have as individuals or organizations are shaped by the metaphors we assign to such designs. For example, if I perceive myself as an optimist, my mental thoroughfares are drawn in large bold lines. I also assume that people will let me change these lines when I believe it is beneficial for others or me. If on the other hand I see myself as a pessimist, the lines are drawn diminutively and I reflect a conservatism that says the lines must always be followed or somehow I will get lost. The metaphors of optimism and pessimism dictate how I view myself, my behavior, and interact with people around me. The same is true for organizations. Metaphors, such as boldness, security, service, education, compassion, and aggressiveness, influence how an organization functions much more than its policies. The metaphors affect the mental models that people have of themselves and the role they play in helping the organization accomplish its mission as a leader. If I can shape the metaphors of a culture, I can then change that culture.

Two major metaphors in denominational culture inform behavior that is ultimately destructive to effectiveness in ministry. The first metaphor is that of shepherd. Obviously, this metaphor is one that is used throughout the entire Scripture, because its reference is the agrarian lifestyle of Israel. The problem is the current image or description that we invest in the term. Our understanding of what shepherds are to be and do, in our congregations, is far more romantic than who shepherds were or what they did in biblical times. Shepherds were entrepreneurs who raised sheep for their livelihood, for food and clothing. Good shepherds led their sheep into green pastures and by still waters in order to obtain three results. They sheared the sheep (not fleeced the flock), ate the sheep, or mated them for reproduction. Sheep were led into zones of comfort in order to be prepared for zones of discomfort. In other words, sheep were expected to produce a profit for the shepherd. The shepherd took care of the sheep, not for the sheep's benefit but for the shepherd's needs. In congregational life our declining institutions think that shepherds take care of sheep for the sheep's benefit, rather then to benefit the Chief Shepherd by accomplishing God's mission. The paradox of Christianity is that sheep are most fulfilled when they are risking life for the Chief Shepherd rather than being pampered by appointed shepherds.

The misunderstanding and misuse of this metaphor has enormous ramifications in local congregations, judicatories, and denominational life. First, the pastor is normally taught that she or he is to function as a shepherd, meaning chaplains to the congregation. We even use the term pastoral care, meaning shepherd care. Most would describe pastoral care as feeding, caring, serving, and meeting the spiritual needs of the sheep. First, this is not the shepherd's job according to Ephesians 4:10-16. It is the responsibility of the congregation to do this work. It is more biblical to speak of congregational care. Mature sheep are to be trained by the shepherds to do this for other sheep. The current situation, however, means that pastors seldom see themselves as leaders while the lay leaders see pastors as individuals who are called to meet their needs, as the pastor's primary task after preaching. And if pastors fail to perform this caring function well, the congregational leaders usually see the pastor as a failure. Consequently, pastors who see the traditional shepherd role as theirs, even if they do it well, will never be able to lead a large number of sheep.

Judicatories often see many of their staff members as shepherds to pastors. Their role is serving pastors, listening to their issues, comforting them, and helping them through times of difficulty. Often those in these judicatory roles have been pastors themselves and are simply reliving with pastors what they saw as their role in congregations. The result is that we recycle a romantic idea of care and help that is neither biblical nor conducive for growth. Often we let pastors know that we want their congregations to grow and be healthy while encouraging them to follow a model of ministry that keeps the congregation relatively small, inwardly focused on its needs, and one that often produces a co-dependent relationship between the pastor and the congregation. Also, if congregations complain to the judicatory about not getting enough care, the pastor is usually the one confronted about the pastor's lack of ministry effectiveness. I am not saying that people should not receive care; rather I am saying that the paradigm we use is both ineffective and unbiblical.

When pastors begin to lead change and move toward health and growth, resistance is raised under the excuse that new commitments of the leader's focus and time will interfere with care ministries. People resist growth by saying we have a hard time caring for our current congregation, if we get more people we will not be able to afford more pastors to care for everyone. Again, the assumption is that care is the pastor's job. The consumer mindset in congregations assumes that the pastor is hired to provide special care for members. It goes with the job because, after all, the pastor is the shepherd.

Most teaching on servant leadership focuses more on servanthood than it does leadership. The assumption is that the pastor must show care (service) to the sheep first, before leadership begins. It is also assumed that leadership, whatever that is, never outweighs the caring aspect of being a shepherd. Often ignored in such teaching is that pastors may be called to serve the people by serving the vision and mission God has, and in doing that the people are served even better.

We suggest to our congregations that the pastor be called the leader. After all, shepherds are called to lead sheep. The leader makes sure the congregation is cared for because sheep do need to be fed, watered, and protected. However, the leader does not perform this caring ministry; the leader equips others to provide the care for sheep. The leader serves the sheep by casting vision, maintaining mission focus, and modeling risk so the sheep will be excited and challenged to resist the enemy, who deserves the metaphor of a roaring lion. Congregations where sheep take on lions and win are congregations filled with excitement that motivates sheep to multipy. We also never use the term pastoral care with congregations, pastors, or other judicatory leaders. The proper term is *congregational care*. It is amazing how change occurs when practices are named properly and then behaviors adjust to fit the new description.

A second biblical metaphor that produces corrupted values is *family*. Not only has it been taken to an unbiblical extreme, but the reference when Westerners use the term *family* is not the description perceived by people in the ancient Mediterranean world. However, the metaphor is an excellent one that has its roots throughout all of Scripture. God speaks as a father to Israel, or as a mother hen who protects her brood, or as a parent who binds the children with cords of love. The New Testament speaks of believers as brothers and sisters, with God as father and Jesus Christ as brother. These are all family images. And while it is true that those in the family of God are to exercise healthy family practices with one another, the primary purpose of the Church is not to be family. The primary image of the congregation is to function as an army, with Jesus Christ, our leader, who attacks the stronghold of Satan. The Church is on a mission and is constantly in a battle for the souls of people. The battle with evil is not only an individual one, for each Christian to wage in her or his daily life. It is the mission of the congregation to be used by God to move women and men from the Kingdom of Darkness to the Kingdom of Light.

Military leaders for thousands of years have learned that soldiers will fight more for comrades than for country, flag, or ideals. Heroes in battle perform courageous acts of foolhardy bravery because they have been trained in small groups where strong famil ial relationships have been developed. Family ties in battle enable the mission to be accomplished as long as soldiers realize that they are on a mission and not attending a family reunion. In this culture we see family as the epitome of human relationships, when in reality the congregation is to be a community on a mission. True community comes together to care for one another as the community accomplishes a purpose. Our current concept of family ends at *care*, with too little thought of what the group will accomplish. Today we see the family promoting individual accomplishment rather than both individual and group accomplishment.

The Christian Church has so imbibed this dysfunctional idea of family, not only at the congregational level but at all denominational levels as well, that we have lost the concept of mission. One reason we are often unwilling to create specific goals and measures of effectiveness is that we know that many in our "family" will not measure up. Yet if we are committed to mission we must tell such people that if they cannot change they can no longer have positions in leadership. Such actions go against our current value of family. We say these people are part of the family so we cannot embarrass them or hurt them. As a result, we let our institutions develop a co-dependent habit of protection, thereby avoiding missional goals that demand accountability.

Professional sports teams that win championships often speak of the relationships between the players as family and how each individual will often go out of her or his way to help another even beyond the demands of the game. Yet each player clearly understands that while such familial relationships exist and affect how they perform, their future with the team depends on performance, not the relationships. Players are traded, retired, cut, benched, or reduced in salary based upon performance, regardless of how much they contribute to the family atmosphere. Players understand and accept such actions because the mission of winning takes precedence over family, even though family values are important and often contribute to winning. Wise coaches often promote the concept and systems related to family relationships. However, these coaches understand the purpose of having a team is to win, not to create competing family reunions each time they face an opponent.

In most congregations and in most judicatories there is little accountability for effectiveness. If accountability exists it occurs in measuring efficiency, even though such efficiency accomplishes little. For example, judicatory staff members may be evaluated on how many pastors they visited, how much conflict mediation they performed, how many church installations they went to, and how many pastors they helped find a placement. Yet all of these tasks can be accomplished without ever affecting the effectiveness of congregations or leading a judicatory in mission.

The family concept also promotes the idea of clerical tenure. Pastors assume that if they have been loyal and faithful soldiers that such behavior over a long time both protects them, in terms of their positions, and gives them authority to speak to any crucial issue facing the judicatory. The controlling principle is not effectiveness in ministry, but tenure in the family. This is one reason why often the more effective pastors that usually have the larger congregations treat judicatories with benign neglect. They understand that family connections are valued more highly than performance. In fact, performance is often seen as a negative value in judicatories since it makes the less effective family members feel guilty.

A final example of how a misplaced view of family affects congregations and judicatories is that it creates separation between those adherents in our family and those adherents in another family. We may laugh and joke about how our denomination is different from another, and we usually know our own weaknesses better than anyone else. However, when it comes to learning from one another about how to be more effective in ministry we usually find it difficult because the other group is not part of the same family. We fail to realize that for the most part effective ministry has nothing to do with denominational or polity distinctions. We are also leery of new people coming into our group, our judicatory, especially if they are effective. As one person in our denomination put it, if we keep letting them in we will lose our distinctiveness and heritage. This statement assumes that everyone in a particular denomination has been there all their lives, which simply is not true. Second, since we have been declining and losing people and congregations, perhaps our distinctiveness and heritage need to be reevaluated by people from the outside. Yet all of this is shaped in the name of *family*. Maintaining relative harmony in the family has become a priority over accomplishing the mission God has set out for congregations.

A Piece of Our Story

I will be telling you our story throughout the book. However, here is a glimpse of what God has done over a period of six years in our judicatory. Perhaps this will encourage you to realize that many of the ideas I will present do come from a new way of thinking and acting in judicatory life. In 1997 the American Baptist Churches of the West, one of thirty-four regions in the American Baptist Churches USA, had 229 congregations located in Northern California and Northwest Nevada. Only thirty-seven, or sixteen percent were growing (the measurement for growth will be described later). The typical congregation was 100 in worship attendance. Pastors and congregations were aging, morale was low, and there was little hope for the future. Missions giving along with congregational attendance had been on the decline for over a decade. There were less than 800 baptisms a year.

In 2002 there were 215 congregations and seventy-two percent of those congregations were experiencing growth. The average attendance in congregations was 188 and there were over 11,000 more people in attendance on Sundays in our congregations than in 1997. Somewhere between 1.2 and 1.5 million new missions dollars had been raised over that period of time and giving to the region was up forty-seven percent. There were over 6,000 baptisms between 1999-2001. The region has eighteen churches that now average over 500 in worship and fifteen of those congregations are led by pastors committed to the region's mission and vision.

God has blessed this judicatory in some amazing ways. Our story has elements that are unique and cannot be replicated. I will identify uniqueness for you. Our story, however, does represent a number of intentional strategies that reflect new ways of thinking and acting as a judicatory. Some of that is possible because of our denomination's polity. Other parts of it are possible in any situation. I will attempt to distinguish what is transferable from that which may take different forms in other kinds of settings.

American Baptist Organization

This book is about the transformation of one denominational judicatory and the transformation of many congregations within that judicatory. This transformation came about because we focused, in a new way, on the local congregation as the basic unit of mission, while emphasizing the importance of leadership. However, our judicatory exists in a larger denominational context with which many may not be familiar. Therefore, I share an overview of that context to explain why we adopted the strategies and tactics to implement transferable principles.

My bias is that denominations will not be reformed from the top. Renewal works its way up from the so-called "organizational bottom." In fact that which is perceived as the "bottom," the local congregation, must again become the entity that is the focus that drives the denomination. Until denominations focus on the local congregation in a new way and embrace true leadership they will continue to become more irrelevant and lose even more support from the adherents within and the observers without.

The American Baptist denomination, like many Protestant denominations in the United States, has much to commend. This denomination excels at its overseas missionary endeavors. It has developed great ministries of justice and compassion in the U.S. It is now a minority-majority denomination in that there are less Euro-American congregations making up the denomination than those from traditional ethnic and racial minorities. The American Baptists have selected a new General Secretary who is bringing a renewed sense of hope and excitement. However, like many other mainline denominations it is declining in numbers and moving toward institutional dysfunction. Therefore, any negative descriptions should be viewed in light of its organizational problems, while recognizing there are rich and rewarding ministries still to be accomplished by American Baptists all around the world.

The American Baptist Churches, USA, is a fellowship of thirty-nine separate corporations connected together by mutual agreement called The Covenant of Relationships. This covenantal agreement, which was entered into voluntarily by each corporation, spells out how these separate organizations work together in mission while working individually to accomplish their own missions.

Thirty-five of the corporations are called regions and the constituents of each region are local congregations. For example, our region, The American Baptist Churches of the West, has 215 congregations or constituents. Those constituents select a board that functions as the trustees of the corporation, known as ABCW. Our region, represented by its board, is then one of the thirty-nine corporations that live out the covenantal agreements articulated in the Covenant of Relationships.

Each regional board, along with the boards of the other thirty-three regions and four national organizations, select representatives to sit on the National Board of ABC-USA. Members of the National Board are then divided into different groups which sit on the boards of the other national corporations that deal with such agendas as international missions, national missions, education etc. In essence representatives to the National Board also sit on at least one other national corporate board, as well as sitting on the board of the region they represent. The chief administrator for the National Board is called the General Secretary and his staff is referred to as the office of the General Secretary. However, the General Secretary has equal standing with the leaders of the other national boards and therefore does not lead or manage the entire denomination.

The leader of the each region has at least two titles. The primary one is Executive Minister of the Region, which means this person functions as the chief administrator for a particular region. The second title is that of Regional Secretary, which means this individual functions as the local regional administrator on behalf of the General Secretary. The Executive Minister is paid by and responsible to the region board while at the same time expected to help carry out the agenda of the National Board, the General Secretary and the General Secretary's staff, as well as the leaders of the other national boards.

Technically, the National Board and its administrative arm, the Office of the General Secretary have no authority over a region or region board, unless it can be demonstrated that the region has in some way violated The Covenant of Relationships. Regions can formally or informally choose to participate in national agendas, whether they come from the General Secretary or another national board. This means that the relationship between the General Secretary and all the regional secretaries is one of influence rather than authority. In this sense each region is autonomous in its relationship with national entities. In some cases the General Secretary or leaders from other national boards may carry a lot of influence through their ability to influence leaders and congregations in a particular region, and through the distribution of discretionary financial resources. In other cases however, the lack of identification with certain national agencies or agendas may increase a region's status with its leaders or congregations or even with other regions.

The American Baptist Churches, USA provides a wide tent which houses a variety of theological, social, and missional agendas and related institutions. Some of these agendas and institutions conflict with each other as they attempt to fulfill their missions. As a result many would argue that American Baptists do not have a common mission or vision. Basic institutional values are not shared or prioritized equally throughout the denomination. And, even American Baptists agree that their denominational structure does not work. The implications resulting from this lack of organizational alignment for local judicatories are two-fold. On the one hand, such confusion produces frustration and breeds low morale. On the other hand, such diversity creates a climate for change, creativity, and the development of newer and more effective ways to do ministry. However, to take advantage of such a climate and implement change requires courage and the willingness to risk. Courage is needed because systemic change breeds suspicion in the rest of the denominational family, since violating perceived family values is considered a greater sin than not accomplishing an effective mission.

Judicatory Life for American Baptists

As stated previously, American Baptists are organized around congregations, regions (middle judicatories), and national denominational entities. The title Executive Minister is used of the leader of the regions. This person has two roles: that of leading and managing the congregations within the region and that of carrying out the agendas set by the General Secretary's office and other national agencies. These two expectations put the Executive Minister in a very interesting situation, especially in a context of conflicting values, competing agendas, a complex structure that often works against itself, and no clear unifying mission or vision. This situation might be described as living in the middle of an hourglass. The national entities, perceived by many as the "top" of the organization, place pressure on the executive and the region to adhere to their agendas, programs, and funding requests, even though they may sometimes compete against each other. Meanwhile local congregations, perceived by many to be at the "bottom" of the organization, demand that the region and its leadership be responsive to their wishes, which at times may agree with certain national agendas while at other times run counter to specific national agendas. The added pressure in most regions is the decline of congregations resulting in declining missions dollars. Fewer missions dollars make it difficult for the congregations to function, the region to serve them, and eventually the ability of national entities to function. All these factors put pressure on the middle of the hourglass where the Executive Minister and region staff members perform. In many cases this pressure produces inertia accompanied by extreme frustration.

We in our region became convinced that such an environment would not be conducive to change, effectiveness, and growth. We believed that the top of the organization, functionally if not perceptually, had to be the local congregation. We needed to do all we could to bring life, transformation, and health to dying congregations even if it meant, for a while, downplaying the role of national denominational life in our region. We believe that if local congregations are not strong and healthy the national denomination is dead, even if it has enough endowment to continue.

In American Baptist life the region is a smaller version organizationally of the national structure or bureaucracy. Local congregations are then often smaller versions of the region in the way they are organized. We believed this too had to change. The metaphor that works for me is that of an archery target. The bullseye in the middle of the target represents the local congregation. The next ring on the target represents the region. Everything the region does focuses on making local congregations healthy, strong, and effective. However, it is important to understand that the ring surrounding the bullseye does not look like the bulls eye. The mission of local congregations should be different from the mission of the regions. Local congregations exist to fulfill the "Great Commission," while regions exist to do three things. Regions exist primarily as catalysts for congregational 1) reproduction and 2) transformation while 3) helping local congregations direct mission dollars. Therefore, since the region's mission is different from its congregations, it structure should be different. We believed that our region should exist to resource, broker for, and network local congregations. Our primary role was not to be the voice of the national denomination to local congregations, particularly when both it and the region were in decline. If we really believe that the local congregation is God's basic and primary unit of mission in the world, then neither we, nor our national denominational entities exist to demand anything of local congregations. Instead we exist to enhance their mission.

Our prayer is that the national denominational entities, which comprise the outer ring of the target, would then be organized to assist regions in meeting their mission. This ring on the target would look different from either the region's ring or the local congregations' bullseye. At this point in our denominational life there is not much evidence that this type of reorganization will occur. Therefore our focus has been the role that our region would play in congregational life by helping individual congregations achieve health through the implementation of this paradigm shift.

Our regional mission is that we exist for the purpose of "Growing Healthy Churches". For such a mission to be accomplished we understand that we must be distinctive in structure and purpose from local congregations while becoming additive to the missions of local congregations, aiding them to become all God would call them to be and do.

There are several implications resulting from this archery mindset, which cause us to function in different ways from many people in other local judicatories. First, we do not function as chaplains to our pastors. We do not expect them to fulfill that role with their congregations, so we demonstrate this behavior in our relationships with the pastors. We do function as mentors, coaches, consultants, trainers, resources personnel, and teachers. This means that our staff must have effective experience in either the transformation of local congregations or evidence of reproducing new ones. It also means that whenever possible we hire people who have led ministries that are larger or more complex in scope than the ministries of the pastors they are working with, so the staff members can help them move to the next level of effectiveness. Regional staff members not only have such a background but are able to effectively communicate what they know and have experienced. They lead pastors and congregations just as they have led effective ministries in the past.

Another implication of fulfilling our mission is that we are willing to confront pastors who are ineffective. We are also willing to confront those congregations and congregational leaders (the emotional terrorists) who for years have chewed up pastors and spit them out. We have confronted both pastors and congregations even though at times it has cost the region the loss of financial support.

Finally, we are adamant about not letting the region be used to promote congregational triangulation, which allows laity to condemn pastors anonymously. If any lay leaders call the region to complain about their pastor those leaders are told they must first confront their pastor before we will become involved in offering assistance, if that is required.

Another implication resulting from this model is that we, as a region, do not promote or conduct conflict mediation. If a congregation wants this done, we will help them find resources in this area to aid them. However, mediation is a ministry the congregation must pay for and is not subsidized by the region. We believe a focus on conflict mediation, which on rare occasions is needed, breeds more conflict mediation while not promoting either health or growth. We say that if you want to grow grass, you do not focus on weeds, instead you focus on growing grass. Congregational transformation will create tremendous conflict in dysfunctional, dying churches. It will be even greater in congregations that perceive themselves as healthy when they are really dying. The worst thing that can happen in the midst of such conflict is mediation, since the conflict is more about the transfer of power and who will lead the congregation, than individuals or groups not being able to get along.

A final implication is that the key role of judicatory staff is to lead pastors and laity to become life-long learners. To do this staff members themselves must be such learners. This means that the majority of staff meeting time, the majority of pastoral cluster time, and the focus of a large portion of the financial investment of the region must be on training, training, and more training. Change in our world is happening so quickly that if we do not keep learning we will be left in the dust.

We have seen God bless many of the major decisions we have made related to change. It has come at great cost at times, but has been worth it. The primary belief we have implemented, with some success and with some failure, is that the local congregation is the basic unit of mission. Many denominational people and agencies say this; however, the issue as with anything else in life is how consistently you practice your belief, especially at the national level. Perhaps it should also be added that if this belief is so, then God expects and assumes that these basic units of mission (congregations) will be healthy, growing, and effectively reproducing as each one seeks to love God and serve neighbor throughout the world.

In the next chapters I unpack the story of our pilgrimage from a region that was unhealthy and dying to one that has changed its practices and is moving toward health once again. The material I share does not imply that we have the all the answers and are doing everything perfectly. We definitely have made a number of significant mistakes along the way. However, we are seeing more and more congregations embrace the values of an outwardly focused mission, reproduction, spiritual vitality, leadership, learning, openness to change, and accountability.

Chapter Two
No Accountability: No Change

A PIECE OF OUR STORY

When I came to the region my role was that of an area consultant with regional responsibilities for training regional staff and developing them as consultants. I soon became involved in developing and implementing regional strategies for working with congregations and pastors. I took on the responsibilities of Executive Minister three years later.

In ABCW each regional consultant (formally called regional minister) was responsible for working with thirty to sixty congregations. After I came we informed this staff of consultants that their future employment with the region would depend not upon how well they serviced their respective congregations but whether the seven to ten congregations they would work with intensely for a year grew in average worship attendance by a minimum of five percent. If most of the seven to ten congregations grew, they would get a raise. If however, the majority failed to grow, they would need to find new employment. At the same time the regional staff were being informed about the new basis for evaluating job performance, the pastors throughout the region were told of two other decisions. First, pastors of non-growing congregations (those that did not average five percent growth in average attendance over at least three years) who left that current congregation would not receive regional assistance or endorsement in locating another congregation within the region. We promised them we would help them find a congregation in another ABC region but not this one. Second, we also communicated that we were asking all congregations, especially those with which our consultants would be spending extra time, to send into the regional Resource Center weekly numbers for congregational attendance, new visitors, baptisms, offerings, new members, leadership training classes, and other numbers. In this chapter I explain how we led individuals and congregations to not only embrace these radical ideas but to value them as crucial.

Due to the systemic decline that the congregations in our region had been facing for over a decade, we knew that we had to perform organizational triage to both stop the decline and help turn congregations around. We also believed that success is related to deciding what it is you want to change, working toward that change, and then figuring out a way to objectively measure whether the change is occurring or not. If it is not occurring, you have no change. However, if some kind of measurement reflects that change has occurred by meeting or surpassing the standard that has been established, you then can declare success. We believed average worship attendance, not membership, was both an important number to measure as well as perhaps the easiest number to get. Therefore we defined growth as a five percent increase in average attendance from one year to the next. If a congregation was experiencing such growth when such had not been happening, we assumed that some healthy changes were occurring. On the other hand, if a congregation remained on a plateau in attendance or continued to decline, it was unhealthy and required change.

We also affirmed that what we take time to count reflects what we value. For example, in a consumer culture individuals over a lifetime spend thousands of dollars while expending thousands of hours simply to keep track of their income, investments, assets, and retirement. Or students seeking entrance into prestigious grad schools harvest college credits with great care and calculate carefully GPA's since these measures are the currency of career advancement. In many denominational and congregational entities there is little counting (other than for budgets), few do ministry accounting, and almost no one is held accountable for anything. This is why many leaders in various positions in church life say that God is primarily interested in faithfulness. We begged to differ with that theology. We wanted to communicate that God is equally interested in fruitfulness along with faithfulness. In John 15 Jesus tells us that obedient disciples bear much fruit.

We knew that we could not (and should not) measure conversions: defined in our theology as individuals moving from sin and darkness into forgiveness and life, through faith in Jesus' substitution ary (atoning) death and resurrection on their behalf. The ministry of salvation requires the work of the Holy Spirit. It is ultimately God's responsibility to accomplish this kind of conversion in the lives of individuals. However, we could measure the practices for which we can take more responsibility. That responsibility is leading a group of people to embrace corporate spiritual health and reject dysfunctional corporate behavior, since it involves corporate disobedience to our Lord. We knew that when congregations began moving from dysfunctional behavior to healthy strategies they grew in worship attendance, which can be measured.

Our grand strategy in turning the region around is to work with seven to ten congregations a year in each area of the region. We ask our consultants to work with those congregations that have the best hope in moving from dysfunction to health in the shortest amount of time. The next year the consultant is to pick the next seven to ten easiest congregations to work with while employing leaders from the congregations that had been helped the previous year to assist the consultant. This process is repeated four times over a period of five years. At the end of five years we had gone from less than twenty percent of our congregations growing to over seventy percent.

The basic principles behind our strategies and tactics are:

1. Fruitfulness is as important as faithfulness.

2. What we count we value.

3. Accountability is a basic requirement for change and must be based upon objective measurement.

Fruitfulness is as important as faithfulness. Often in the Christian life we value fruitful labor for God whether there are results or not. The value is in the service itself. For example, as I was growing up in church I heard regularly that any effort was worth doing even if only one person's life was changed. Often prior to our "annual revival services" our pastor would say that all the work and preparation was worth it, even if only one person made a decision to follow Jesus. As I got older I found myself asking the question, What if we expended the same amount of effort differently and as a result observed ten decisions to turn around, wouldn't that be better? For years missionaries were lauded for faithful services in difficult cultures where there was seldom any responses to their efforts. They were faithful. However, missions experts today realize that often these missionaries presented eternal truth in ways that were culturally irrelevant or even culturally offensive. We have often confused the method of ministry with the nature of the message, and when there have been no results we have honored the faithfulness of the messenger.

I recognize that spiritual results are ultimately the work of the Holy Spirit. About that the Bible is abundantly clear. It is also quite clear that God does expect and honor servants for their faithfulness. However, the biblical text is also quite clear that God has high expectations for stewards who will be held accountable for how well they have produced spiritual dividends from the investments God has given. The text is also clear that we must be wise in understanding how we communicate the message. So we let the message offend, if that is the case, not the method by which we present that message. This principle forced us to create new metaphors for our regional staff members and our pastors. We asked pastors to forget that they are pastors and think of themselves as missionaries. Behaviors and priorities are changed when the leader sees the culture as "pagan" and opposed to the Gospel message, with the local congregation functioning as a mission outpost designed to reach that culture. We also defined leaders as people who actually had other people following them. Leadership ceased to be a position and became a function. Regional staff became consultants, which communicated expertise and resource, rather than chaplain and denominational ambassador. The label used for the regional office was changed from "Regional Office" to "Resource Center," which indicated a whole new reason for existing, and took priority over the administrative and management functions conducted there.

This principle then led us to develop new strategies. One was a redeployment of regional staff. Another was to create new expectations for pastoral leaders. We also began to create new expectations for congregations and congregational leaders. The job of the pastor and congregational leaders was to lead the congregation to accomplish a mission of changing a community first rather than meeting the consumer demands of fickle congregations which would then often be willing to help others once their needs were met.

What we count we value. Most congregations write an annual report that is given to the congregation (and judicatory). This report, for which there is no set form in Baptist circles, recounts what occurred in the congregation over the past year, in each major area of ministry in the congregation. A budget report and the new budget are usually included along with statistics on baptisms and conversions. There is usually a letter or report from the pastor, and other staff members in multiple staff congregations. Most of the sections are then written by either the staff member or a lay leader overseeing a particular ministry area.

In the late 1990s you would see just a part of the year's activity, other than a reporting of statistics and finances, numbers about events, meetings, meals, and the names of committee or team members overseeing ministries with notations of thanks for their participation as volunteers. The relational aspects of congregational life is counted because family is valued over mission. Not reported were the effectiveness of evangelism strategies (usually little if anything was being done in evangelism), the number of new leaders being developed, the number of new small groups being created, along with the number of leaders being developed to lead the new groups, total visitors and the percentage of visitors cultivated for membership, new disciples, the number of people and dollars it was taking to produce new disciples, and so forth. Since the congregations did not see themselves as missional in nature they did not count those things that reflected mission, rather they counted that which was important to them, namely relationships and those ministries that fostered relationships.

Our strategy was to change that which received a higher priority in terms of value. Obviously relationships are important, but relationships are not the primary purpose for local congregations existing, just as sports teams do not exist so the team members can develop a sense of family.

Accountability is a basic requirement for change and must be based upon objective measurement. We are creatures of habit. Therefore to introduce systemic change into an organization that has been functioning one way for years, even for people who embrace the change intellectually, demands accountability to make sure the change is being implemented. This accountability must be done with some objective measurement in mind in order to clearly demonstrate that people are either practicing the change or ignoring or avoiding it. Therefore, part of our strategy is to express what the change looked like in order to communicate what was acceptable and what was unacceptable. We then articulate some form of measurement to determine whether acceptable change was occurring. The ways we expressed what was acceptable and unacceptable and the ways we measured became the tactics.

Changed Expectation Demands Resources to Reach Expectations

If we expect pastors and congregations to be held accountable, we as leaders must be held accountable. So we redeployed regional staff, expressed how the roles of regional staff members would change, both personally and in their role as resources for pastors and congregations, and how the effectiveness of the resulting changes would be measured, thus introducing accountability.

First we changed the title of *area minister* to *area consultant*. Prior to this change each area minister was responsible to oversee thirty to sixty local congregations. These individuals fulfilled a number of traditional roles. They functioned as chaplains to local pastors, often meeting with them to offer counsel and advice while the pastors shared their frustrations at attempting to oversee declining and increasingly dysfunctional congregations. The area ministers also represented the region at ceremonial events in the life of congregations, such as anniversaries, new pastor installations, and ordinations. They worked with search committees to help locate new pastors, led monthly pastoral clusters, and often acted as conflict mediators when congregations were fighting.

In our region, an area minister's evaluation was based on a maintenance model. By this I mean that each staff member was asked to perform certain behaviors. As long as these behaviors were performed well staff members were deemed effective even though congregations continued to decline. They reported the number of congregations and pastors they visited each month, the number of ceremonial events in which they participated, and the hours spent with search committees or in conflict mediation. However, they were not held accountable for whether the congregations under their oversight grew or diminished in size. No connection was made between their faithful service and fruitfulness in the lives of pastors or congregations. They were not held accountable for whether evangelism was taking place or not or how many new converts were being baptized, or even if baptisms were no longer occurring in a Baptist church. There was no expectation to increase or help raise new missions dollars in congregations. Yet most congregations across the region were aging, numbers of both people and dollars were declining, and the overall health and vitality of the region was becoming lost and assumed to be part of a former grand tradition. The area ministers were faithfully fulfilling their responsibilities yet no significant fruit was being produced. Nor was there any expectation that they might be held accountable to help produce such fruit.

Changing a person's title from area minister to area consultant does not make that individual a consultant. In fact the area ministers in place at the time had no idea what it meant to be a congregational consultant. Those individuals saw themselves as chaplains and mediators. They had no idea how to help a congregation become healthy or grow. Most had never led a congregation to growth and health (and this was one reason they were in judicatory or denominational work) and they were ignorant of most of the voices who are writing about congregational health, congregational growth, changing organizations, or missional thinking.

However, changing their title did several things. First, it changed the metaphor of the role, which is far more important than changing any policy. Calling these people consultants created a whole new set of expectations for themselves and others. The new expectations moved these individuals from places of comfort about their roles to a deep feeling of inadequacy. Second, it communicated to the region staff members that not only was their role changed, and along with it the expectations for success, but so too was the very nature and existence of the region. What had been valued before and rewarded accordingly would no longer be saluted. Third, it also communicated to congregations that the region's relationship with them was changing. Most pastors and congregations did not understand the implications of the change immediately. This change however, was the initial step in demonstrating that the region viewed its primary task as assisting and providing resources for congregations in order to have them regain health and as a result begin growing again.

As leaders in the region we were now faced with a major task. By changing the title of area minister to area consultant, accompanied by new expectations, we now had the moral obligation to provide these individuals with the resources required to accomplish their new responsibilities and meet the new expectations. Therefore, we chose to attack this problem with two tactics. First, we created a steep learning curve in order to help the new consultants get up to speed on the issues, ideas, principles, strategies, and tactics related to congregational transformation. Secondly, we created a mentoring model enabling the new consultants to become congregational consultants.

The first step in creating the steep learning curve was to change staff meetings from one- day to two-day events. This enabled us to spend a day and a half on training. Staff members were given books and tapes related to health, growth, change, and leadership to become informed prior to meetings. (The training materials were produced by writers and speakers from the Christian world and the business world.) Then each month staff member training focused on one major issue derived from the assigned material. An example of topics for staff meetings would be discussions related to levels of leadership, breaking the 200 barrier, developing mission and casting vision, and so forth. We also brought in key trainers from across the country to lead staff meetings from time to time. Sometimes we held extended retreats for staff members and key pastors in order to broaden exposure to national leaders. One example was with George Bullard, who was brought in to teach the concept of lifecycles in congregations and demonstrate how this tool can be used to leverage change. Staff member training continues on to the present because of our commitment to be life long learners.

The second tactic was to create a mentoring program for staff members to learn how to consult with congregations. As a congregational consultant for over fifteen years, I developed the mentoring strategy. I first taught our staff members about the entire consulting process from both a broad philosophical perspective to the specific implementation of consulting strategies. We used case studies from actual congregations in order to give people the opportunity to wrestle with specific implementation tactics. I then provided a basic model we would use with our congregations. It was flexible enough to adapt to different kinds of congregations, with unique needs or situations, that might also need a consultation accomplished in a time frame different from the norm. However, the basic structure we followed looked like this:

- The congregation was assessed through the use of one or two specific tools we decided as a region to adopt.

- A region staff member spent a weekend with the congregation dealing with the results surfaced by the assessment tools.

- A region staff member met each month with the pastor, board, and/or other leaders to implement recommendations coming from the consultation.

On months when there was one big meeting with all the parties involved and other months there were a number of individual meetings with different persons or groups. These monthly meetings lasted for a minimum of one year. (See Chapter 4 for the entire consultation process, including information about why we chose the tools.)

Our commitment was to work with the area ministers already on region staff to help them become consultants. I think our change could have happened even more quickly if we would have changed certain staff positions first. However, part of the miracle is that we saw the change with the area consultants that were already in place. Those who hung in there and stayed with the program faced major readjustments personally and professionally in order to survive. To their credit they made the changes and did succeed.

I conducted over fifty congregational consultations myself in the first three years as we employed this new strategy. During staff meetings I would train or provide training for our consultants related to congregational consulting. On each consultation I would take one or two consultants with me. My selection of consultants was based generally on two criteria. First, I selected the consultant in whose area the congregation existed, since this consultant would be working with this congregation each month during the year after the weekend consultation. I selected the second consultant based upon the degree of difficulty it would take to work with a particular congregation. I wanted the consultants with the best aptitude for consulting to work with the more difficult congregations so they would be better prepared to work with similar congregations when they were on their own.

During their first experience the staff members would observe the application of the tools and the entire weekend of consultation. We would debrief when the consultation was over and deal with observations and questions they might have. I would then hand off the monthly implementation meetings to the consultant responsible for congregations in that area. However, I would coach them in preparation for their monthly meetings with the pastor and other leaders. The second time the consultant joined me for a consultation he or she would take on pieces of the process they felt comfortable handling. Primarily the consultant conducted the third consultation, while I participated as a coach and mentor. After those three experiences each consultant was expected to handle the majority of consultations in the area for which the consultant was responsible. I remained available for coaching and mentoring assistance as consultants conducted their own consultations. I continued to consult with larger congregations or those with major issues or severe conflicts. However, even in those situations I always involved the consultant in that congregation's area and we did the consultation as a team.

Within a year, most of the consultants were conducting consultations on their own. Obviously some were better at it than others. In that light consultants often helped each other and some would go into another's area and do a particularly difficult consultation for him or her. In some cases where there was severe conflict, consultants switched so the consultant coming in could function as the prophet and the consultant who would work with the congregation on a monthly basis would be seen as the leader bringing up good change strategies. By this time the monthly training became even more relevant as consultants would interact with the material in relation to the congregations where they were consulting. The learning related to leadership, congregational health, and church growth was no longer abstract. Rather staff members were being forced to develop specific implementation strategies for congregations with which they were consulting, related to the principles they were learning.

Moving from a Maintenance Model to a Faithfulness/Fruitfulness Model

As we changed the paradigm from area minister to area consultant we knew we needed to make three other significant changes to enable the paradigm to work. First, we relieved staff members from current expectations. Therefore, we told them that they would no longer be evaluated and compensated for how many meetings they had with pastors or congregations. They were not even expected to visit with every pastor or congregation every year, which incidentally some pastors found as blessing, while some saw it as abandonment. There were some who probably did not care one way or another. Perhaps those pastors who felt abandoned, felt that way because they no longer had anyone to share their complaints about small, declining, and frustrating congregations. These pastors were disappointed at the lack of communication. They were also frustrated since they no longer felt validated or affirmed by the region. All of these feelings raised a number of complaints. However, we knew that if we were going to change expectations for staff members (as well as congregations and pastors) and introduce staff members to a new kind of accountability we could not keep doing ministry the same way. Doing it the same way would produce the same results, while adding new responsibilities and expectations on top of previous expectations would produce frustration for staff members. It would also guarantee that they would be ineffective at both the old way and the new way.

Second, we let region staff members know what the new expectations were and how they would be implemented. Each consultant was to pick seven to ten congregations with which each would work intensely through the end of the following year. Each congregation would go through a consultation and the consultant would work intensely with the leaders, meeting each month to implement new strategies to produce health and growth. We in essence guaranteed congregations that if they would take seriously what we were offering, and work hard at implementing the ideas being presented, they would see a five percent increase in average worship attendance over the previous year. I would tell congregations if we cannot help you, then you should consider not sending more missions dollars; however if we do help you, we will be asking for more. The consultant therefore would be evaluated at the end of first year in relation to the number of growing congregations out of the seven to ten being helped and the increase of new missions dollars coming into American Baptist missions. Again, growth was defined as a five percent increase in average worship attendance over the previous year. This first experience with these congregations was an experiment. No consultant would lose employment if the majority of congregations with which they were working were not growing or generating new missions dollars. However, there would be an accounting to see how well they as consultants were functioning. The reason for this was that they would be expected to select a new seven to ten congregations to work with in the second year. How well those congregations were doing or not doing at the end of the year in relation to growth and giving would impact the consultant's raise and or employment with the region. At the end of the second full year some staff changes were made because of the inability of some to meet the criteria.

It was important that the consultants knew they would not be compensated for how well they conducted their monthly cluster meetings with groups of pastors. However, we were able to get most of the consultants to understand, the better the training, the higher the respect they would have in the eyes of pastors, and the more credibility they would receive to lead congregational transformation. Their evaluation would be based upon the number of congregations that moved from dysfunction to health and as a result started growing. The cluster was to be viewed as an opportunistic platform to be used to earn the right to lead congregations through change.

The area consultants were in the process of becoming effective congregational consultants. These changes also demonstrated that what we would be asking of both congregations and pastors we had first asked of ourselves. It also modeled that we would resource people in order to enable them to meet new expectations. In our Baptist setting with autonomous congregations that are mostly free to do as they decide, we could not demand accountability. We needed to lead people to embrace it for themselves.

Pastors and Accountability

As worship attendance decreases in congregations, average ages of congregations increase. The average age of pastors across the region was increasing as well. Probably one quarter of the pastors were at or nearing retirement age. This, by the way, turned out to be a blessing, since many who could not handle the extreme paradigm shift were able to retire with dignity and honor. There were few young pastors in the region, since this area of the country is a wonderful place to live and as a result pulpits are in demand. Many of the current pastors had been rotating among a number of the congregations over the years. A basic value that most held was that if a pastor was perceived as a "loyal soldier" that pastor would always be helped by the region to find a new pastorate when she or he felt that one's ministry was over with the current congregation. This help would be forth coming whether the current congregation was healthy and growing or dysfunctional and dying. As a result pastors stayed in one place approximately five years and then moved on to another congregation.

We had to make a statement to get the attention of the pastors. Therefore, while in the process of changing regional staff expectations, we communicated that the region would no longer help any pastor find another pastorate in the region if the congregation they were leaving was not growing. We would offer them some help to find a congregation to pastor in one of the other thirty-three American Baptist regions, but not this one. As almost anyone can imagine, this announcement was met with shock and disbelief. It was said this was no way for a region to act and it was a violation of one of its very purposes for existing. There was even more anger when pastors actually found out that we meant it and would not and did not help them locate other congregations to pastor in the region. Having said this we knew that Baptist congregations can do whatever they want in calling a pastor and could go around us if they so desired. A few congregations and pastors did just that. However, most congregations, upon learning that we would not recommend a candidate and discovering that this person had not seen any congregations grow under his or her leadership, usually backed away. This was especially true when we revealed what we would do for them in helping them find a pastor that could lead them to health and growth. How we helped congregations locate effective pastors is explained in Chapter 5.

However, once this decision was made, it took frequent and redundant communication to help both pastors and congregations, who had learned of it, to understand it. With the pastors we had to assure them that we would not leave them in a lurch. We would stand by them and help them grow and develop as leaders if they wanted to pursue that course. Our goal was not to lose pastors over this decision but have them step up to the task of being a leader who would take risks and be willing to be held accountable for fruitful ministry. We also assured them that if they took such risks the region was not going to abandon them. In the past when congregations had conflicts, it was often easier to have the pastor leave, and the region was known for advocating this. We knew that change would bring conflict, and we assured the pastor that when the conflict came, we would help the pastor deal with the dragons in the congregation who did not want health and growth because it affected their ability to hold influence in the congregation. As we modeled our words and pastors saw consistency between what we said and did, they began to buy into the concept of staying and helping their congregations become healthy and grow.

However, we were also honest with the pastor. If we felt that the pastor, after diligent efforts and time for seeing results, did not have the ability or gifts to lead, we then told the pastor we thought that she or he should leave. However, in such cases we helped the pastor work out a healthy departure both emotionally and financially, and helped as best we could with relocation elsewhere in the nation.

We found that this decision resonated with many in the congregation who understood that for them to survive in their livelihood they must be accountable. Finally, someone was willing to say the same thing in the religious world. Those who struggled with it the most at either the clergy or lay level were those who placed the value of family above the value of accomplishing the mission that Jesus Christ has given his church.

Providing Pastoral Resources for New Expectations

Having stated this new expectation for pastors, we knew we must now provide resources to enable them to lead their current congregations to health and growth. In many cases the problem was not the pastor's ability or inability to lead. The problem was broader and more systemic. Seminaries and denominational systems do not teach or train people to do effective ministry or be leaders. (I do not believe that leadership development should be the job of seminaries, even though most claim to do it while ignoring the reality that they do not.) However, leader development should be a top priority for judicatories even though they do not do it or even profess to do it. Therefore, we as a region took on the responsibility of training our pastors to be effective leaders of healthy growing congregations. We undertook this training process on our own and did not enlist any outside help from other institutions including seminaries.

We believe that the human key to congregational transformation usually begins with the pastor. As a result we entered into an intensive training program for pastors, lay leaders, and congregations. (I will discuss how this was funded later). We put on a region-wide training event every quarter for three years. We brought in speakers such as Leith Anderson, John Maxwell, Stan Toler, Herb Miller, George Bullard, Kennon Challahan, Glen Martin, and Randy Frazee. During the first two years the training was focused primarily on leadership. We wanted pastors to know how leaders functioned and behaved, and that one of their primary tasks is to disciple and develop new leaders. We also made sure that one training event a year related to issues surrounding money. Again, we want pastors to know how to increase giving, how to do financial stewardship well, and become responsible for raising the dollars to support the missions and visions being developed in their respective congregations. All of these events are open to all our pastors while many were designed for pastors, lay leaders, and congregational members. We also offered scholarships to anyone in the region who wanted to attend training related to these topics being held elsewhere in the country. So, for example, for over four years we provided scholarships for hundreds to attend the "Purpose Driven Church" conference conducted by Saddleback Church in Southern California.

The second way we began to resource pastors in order to help them develop as effective leaders was to change the way we did monthly pastoral clusters. As I already mentioned, we added a significant training component to the event. However, there was another important aspect that must be understood about the training piece. We knew that when pastors go to large training events they seldom ever change. They may want to change and may have completely bought into that which was taught at the seminar. However, the pressures they face upon returning home, or more importantly an inability to know where to begin to make changes, often means that nothing happens and the event is simply another notebook on the pastor's shelf. In light of this phenomenon we designed much of our training in clusters to provide hands-on ways to implement pieces of a recent training event that required the pastors to report at the next cluster meeting about how they had implemented change in their local setting. The reporting time developed accountability while producing a peer-learning environment where pastors could interact over the principles they had learned and the wisdom needed to implement them in each respective context. Our intent was to provide a positive, supportive, and encouraging learning environment for pastors. This implementation piece is crucial in producing change. I believe all the other training we did would not have amounted to much if we had not held pastors accountable for actual changes through our cluster system.

A third way we began to resource pastors, as well as congregations, was to change the image and role of our regional office. We changed the terminology from Region Office to Regional Resource Center. We purchased thousands of dollars worth of books, tapes, and workbooks on leadership, congregational health and growth, culture, and change. We purchased curriculum related to specific ways to do ministry in fundraising, assimilation, and helping new people become disciples in the local congregation. We purchased series of sermons from some of the leading pastors in the country that could be used by our pastors as another resource in sermon preparation. Every time we had a speaker come into our region we purchased books the speaker had written and had them available at the event. If the speaker mentioned certain books that had changed the way the speaker did ministry we announced at the seminar that we would be buying them and making them available. We are now adding numerous materials related to the role of spouses. We are particularly concerned about what happens to them as their mates lead congregational change from dysfunction to health. All the materials we purchased were, and to this day are, put into catalogues we produce and made available to pastors and congregations through loaning or made available for sale at our cost. Even though we still do region business at our Resource Center it is viewed far more by many of our pastors as a place for resources and study. A number of them spend one day a quarter at the Resource Center studying, preparing sermons, or examining and reviewing ministry resources.

A fourth resource pastors now had was access to a newly trained regional staff. Prior to our intervention most pastors would not have seen staff members as a resource particularly in producing healthy growing congregations. If anything they would have been seen as a detriment. Now as staff members were climbing their severe learning curve and being mentored in consulting, they were becoming great resources for many pastors. Even if a staff member could not be the resource to the pastor that staff member knew where to locate the resource and as a result functioned as a broker for the pastor.

Another facet that related to staff members as a resource to pastors was our commitment to only hire new regional staff members who were already leaders and who had already demonstrated effectiveness and growth in previous ministries. This is a difficult task since most effective pastoral leaders do not see denominational work as a viable, fulfilling, or interesting option. Filling the positions required the continual hard work of networking.. Finding qualified staff is difficult but getting them to consider such employment as an option is even more difficult. It means painting a vision of what is and what will happen, while assuring them of a working environment that will be creative, open, challenging, and free from most denominational hassles. I have found that you need to convince people that such ministries done well will enhance their ability to expand their influence for the Kingdom of God beyond what even one large congregation can accomplish.

I see us molding a team. The metaphor is probably best demonstrated by a baseball team, where the team is enhanced as each individual member is somewhat selfish about padding his or her own statistics. I want to hire all-stars who have the freedom to create and develop their own areas of ministry. My job is simply to keep them on target in accomplishing the mission and achieving the vision. I also see my role as keeping all the denominational "stuff" away from them as much as possible so they can fulfill their roles without worrying about such things. I and the support staff will handle the denominational responsibilities, and in comparison to others, our region has one of the more ambitious plans for fulfilling our national denominational goals.

Two examples are our current Missions Support Person and our Church Planting Director. Our Missions Support person has a seminary degree, has been a pastor, has managed millions of dollars working for a major investment firm, and is always in demand from other organizations as a fundraiser. Our Church Planting Director has planted two congregations by himself, the last one going from zero to six hundred in attendance. Our pastors see these people along with other new staff members as valuable resources to the region. Regional positions in our judicatory are no longer offered to former pastors who found it difficult in the parish.

Probably sixty percent or more of the pastors who were in place when we began the intervention were still leading the same congregations after six years. These pastors learned that leadership in the region was going to hold them accountable for healthy growing congregations. If they did not want to accept this they either needed to leave the region or remain in their own setting, generally passed over from much of the life and interaction of the region. As a result most of the pastors, over sixty percent, stepped up to the task.

Holding Congregations Accountable

We knew that health and growth would not come if only regional staff members and pastors were held accountable. We also hold congregations accountable. Holding congregations accountable means holding the leaders of congregations accountable. Tremendous change can occur in a short amount of time when both the pastors and lay leaders are in agreement about making changes and are committed to not allowing individuals within the congregation to drive wedges between them collectively or individually. Therefore, we knew we had to develop tactics that would enable us to help hold congregations accountable for changes that would result in health and growth. We also knew that to attract them to this accountability we could not command them to follow our wishes.

The congregation was held accountable through reporting of statistics related to numerical, financial and program growth. Forms were created that had to be filled out each week. These forms asked for attendance, giving, conversions, baptisms, new visitors, return visitors, small group meetings, and leadership training. Congregations could fax, email, or call an 800 number to report each week. If the report did not appear, someone at the Resource Center contacted the pastor or the consultant to obtain it. These reports were published for anyone to have and were used at cluster meetings to encourage, celebrate, and hold pastors and their congregations accountable. In the first year the region was getting reports from over fifty congregations. The next year the region was getting over one hundred reports from around the region since the congregations that had been worked with in the previous year were still reporting along with the new congregations.

We defined success and then found ways to measure that success, to determine whether it was being achieved or was just chatter. Other measurements could be used. The ones we chose have limitations and do not reflect all of congregational life and the making of true disciples.[1] But as a beginning point it enabled us to get the attention of the potential leaders in dysfunctional and dying congregations. It enabled us to state our mission, our vision, and measure whether we are moving toward it or away from it. I believe God blessed us in part because we were willing to find a way, even an imperfect one, to be held accountable and demonstrate fruitfulness along with faithfulness. We have taken and continue to take the Great Commission seriously enough to enforce mutual accountability for our behaviors.

As a denominational executive I cannot take responsibility for each declining congregation. It is not my job to help a particular congregation move from dysfunction to health. However, when the majority of congregations are declining and therefore the judicatory is declining, that is my responsibility. As the leader, I should be held accountable and hold accountable those over whom I have influence to see that we move from dysfunction to health. Failure to accept this challenge is to fail in my part of fulfilling Jesus' Commission to the church.

---

[1] For example, as one way to measure accountability inside a congregation, in the earliest days of John Wesley's movement, individuals were held accountable in small group covenants for acts of mercy (e.g., visiting prisons) and acts of piety (e.g., prayer). Those who did not show evidence of these practices were asked not to return.

Chapter Three
Leadership * Leadership * Leadership

A PIECE OF OUR STORY

Two new leaders came to the region of the American Baptist Churches of the West. The first leader, the new Executive Minister, replaced a man who had served in that position for twenty-five years. During the former executive's tenure much had been done to build the region into a strong entity supported by excellent financial resources. However, during the last ten years of his term the region and congregations had declined to a point where many of the financial resources were being used simply to keep the ship afloat. The last two years of his tenure were marked by a bitter battle among congregations and pastors about the issue of homosexuality. His retirement coincided with four congregations being asked to leave the region because of their commitment to affirm homosexuality as a legitimate biblical lifestyle.

The new Executive Minister arrived, followed by my arrival as his first hire two months later. Within a year a number of amazing events occurred. The constituents of the region (the congregations) had voted to put most of the region's by-laws in abeyance (by-laws are legislated documents that determine how a region functions); the congregations also voted to release two of the four million dollars in savings to be spent over three years for leadership development and the recruitment of growth oriented pastors; regional staff, key pastors, and certain congregations were being held accountable for moving from dysfunction to health and growth; a strategy with measurable goals was in place to help turn congregations around one at a time; a new strategy for locating, recruiting, and helping congregations find growth oriented pastors was in place; thousands of new missions dollars were being raised; area ministers had become area consultants and were being trained to consult with congregations; the region was becoming a mission and vision led organization rather than an institutionally driven one; congregations were adopting a prayer ministry geared to producing change and an outward focus; and leadership, training, and life-long learning were quickly becoming regional values.

From a human viewpoint all of these changes went back to leadership and new leaders. We as a region were quickly learning that all we did was related to either good leadership or poor leadership.

If leadership is as crucial as people are saying, in the non-Christian world and the Christian one, then people in authority over judicatories need to re-examine who leads them. For years, pastors and church leaders have blamed followers for the problems in the church. It is time that we who are leaders look inward and admit that the problem is "us." Perhaps it is time to say that even the requirement for religious leaders needs to change. Although the Old Testament prophets and Jesus had a lot to say about the people of Israel who were disobedient, ultimately it was the leaders who were held accountable. The New Testament speaks of the gift of leadership and most, if not all, of the New Testament epistles were written to leaders. The assumption of the biblical writers is that the leaders would bring about the changes they were addressing in their epistles. If people are not following then either we are not leading as we are capable, we do not know how to lead, or we simply are not leaders and need to step away from leadership positions. Leadership has at least one simple test: Is anyone following or not?

Leadership in one sense is amoral. It can be use to lead people to great achievements, such as those who led thirteen colonies to independence and nationhood. It can also be used to produce great evil, such as Adolph Hitler. For us, in our region, good leadership was described as faithful disciples producing good fruit, defined as renewed congregations, the multiplication of disciples, the development of pastoral leaders who in turn produced more leaders, and a judicatory that functioned missionally. We knew that new leaders were leading because there was tangible fruit that could be measured. People were following and as a result old behaviors were discarded and new behaviors reflecting new ways of thinking were adopted.

In this chapter I examine the experience judicatory leaders need to function. I then discuss how leaders in judicatories need to move judicatories from organizational dysfunction to spiritual and organizational health, vitality, growth and reproduction. After all it is not enough to find good leaders, but we mujst find leaders who have the courage to perform, the wisdom to know what foundational principles need to be adopted, and the insight to implement effective strategies.

The Changing Church and Non-changing Judicatories

Congregations continue to change and morph in relation to culture just as they have for 2,000 years. In our culture we are observing a pattern where more and more people are attending fewer and fewer congregations. The same thing that is happening with congregations is also occurring in school systems, businesses, farming, and supermarkets. Although the small congregation as a remnant of an agrarian culture still persists, it is not small congregations where the majority of people attend. More and more Americans are attending congregations that offer them options, anonymity, particular ministries geared to targeted family needs, and opportunities for service that are varied, different, and challenging. I will not attempt here to provide the reasons for such change nor critique whether this change is generally positive or negative. However, it is thoroughly accurate to say in the United States that the sum of people who attend larger congregations is greater than the sum of those who attend smaller ones. This development is denied by some denominational leaders who would prefer to maintain the numbers of small congregations who are consumers of products, services, and pastors.

Leadership skills required to lead and direct larger congregations are vastly different from those required to lead smaller ones. Larger congregations are not simply smaller congregations that now have more people attending. Instead, they are different organizational and social entities, requiring specialization. A large department store is very different from a small one-person boutique, and it demands different skills of those leading it. So too is a large congregation in relation to a small one.

It is extremely important to concede that large and small congregations can be either healthy or unhealthy. However, in North America most small congregations are small and remain that way because they are spiritually and organizationally dysfunctional. Many large congregations have become large as a result of pursuing organizational health and in many cases spiritual health as well. If small congregations are truly healthy they will not remain small, but will grow and reproduce in one way or another. If a large congregation becomes unhealthy, it will eventually decline. We must be clear that size in congregations, like growth in children, is related to health or illness. However, while size often indicates health, again as we may remember with children, size can mask significant potential disease.

The problem with judicatories is that they are often run with small and dysfunctional congregational mentality by people with experience limited to leading small, dysfunctional congregations. Therefore the focus of judicatories is often on the congregations that are small, unhealthy, dysfunctional, and headed toward death. These kinds of congregations are all the leaders know how to lead, because of the their previous experiences within the system. The focus of such leaders is too often on the congregations that have the least resources and are no longer the strength of the denomination. I seldom meet pastors of large congregations in other judicatories or denominations who tell me that they are seen as positive examples by their judicatory leaders or other pastors within their judicatory.

The real need in judicatory leadership is for individuals who have taken small, dysfunctional congregations and led them to become healthy, larger, vital congregations. Such individuals understand the change and transition processes. They are sensitive to the steps and stages of growth. They have learned which hills to die upon and which battles to fight another day. They know the difference between health and dysfunction, false piety and true spirituality, single-cell organisms and complex structures, leadership and management. Like most congregations in North America, regardless of size, most judicatories are dysfunctional, dying entities that need to be renewed, given hope, and provided leadership that will produce health and growth.

Consider some examples of the differences between large congregational thinking and small congregational thinking. In many larger congregations commitment to the mission of the congregation and pursuing the vision takes precedence over all other concerns, desires, and interests. In fact, individuals, groups, and even people in authority are asked to submit their agendas and desires to the mission and vision that the leaders believe God has given to that particular congregation. This is usually not true in smaller congregations. In these congregations there is usually a multiplicity of missions and visions, and different individuals or cliques are championing their own at the expense of common missions and visions. Also, the needs of individuals usually take precedence over the mission and vision when they come into conflict, since "family" is a key value. This is often why smaller congregations stay small and become unhealthy. It also is apparent when large congregations experience sudden decline. Their focus is on what is best for those within the congregation as opposed to those for whom the congregation is responsible, the community outside of the congregation.

Larger congregations generally place an emphasis on leadership and the leaders. They have learned how to give their leaders both the responsibility for ministry and the authority to get the task accomplished while holding them accountable. The emphasis is far more on the results that are expected than the process in obtaining those results. Leaders have the freedom to see that the mission is being accomplished and the vision is being reached, even if it means sacrifices for them and the congregation. The job of leaders is to lead and equip the laity to do the work of ministry. In smaller congregations the emphasis is more on the process of making decisions, being assured that relationships are not hurt and that everyone has a say. Usually in smaller congregations the pastoral leaders are given the responsibility to perform ministry, while the laity assume authority over the ministry. Larger congregations tend to trust their leaders, while smaller ones tend to control them.

A final example is that leaders in larger congregations understand that the large congregation is a series of complex interdependent systems made up of many interlocking subsystems, which, when working together, function well and accomplish a mission and vision. However, a change in one part of any system affects the whole.

Judicatories tend to be led by individuals with small congregational experience and thinking. The leaders are often much more concerned about keeping the institution going than accomplishing a mission, or assume they can accomplish a mission with an aging bureaucracy that inhibits change. There is no attempt to let the mission, what ever it may be, control decisions, events, or the multitude of agendas present in any judicatory.

There is a lack of emphasis on leadership, particularly the kind of leadership that promotes change and suggests that the current way of functioning is not only ineffective but foolish. Usually the leaders who push the envelope and try new paradigms are marginalized and not given the freedom to fail with honor. I am told constantly by many in other judicatories that "our judicatory" spends far too much time with the smaller, hurting, and disgruntled congregations, while ignoring the larger, growing congregations. I believe such behavior is related to corrupted views of the biblical metaphors of shepherd and family. However, this behavior also is practiced because leaders of judicatories do not have successful and effective experience with large congregational thinking.

Judicatory leaders also tend to honor their particular denomination's way of working, even though the structures often reflect rural thinking that in some cases may derive from seventeenth-century Europe, when their ancestors arrived as immigrants. These leaders also want to make sure that every voice is heard. There is a failure to understand that, while every person is equal in his or her standing with and before God, not every voice carries equal weight.

Finally many judicatory leaders do not understand that their judicatory is a complex, interlocking, interdependent series of systems, with many subsystems that cannot be tinkered with apart from the whole—if the goal is missional change. Rather, the entire system must be overhauled. New systems and subsystems need to be created if the institution is going to move from dysfunction to missional endeavor. It is not merely a matter of stating a mission and creating a vision. New values based on foundational principles must be embraced, new strategies reflecting those values must be implemented, and new structures must be created to allow the new strategies to be implemented. Such thinking is reflected in many larger congregations while not even being considered in smaller ones.

A New Kind of Leadership for Judicatories

If I am right that judicatories are selecting their leaders from smaller congregational experiences, at least during most of their pastoral career, which is contributing to the lack of appropriate leadership, then we must state a fundamental way to end this instinct.

When the new Executive Minister and I came to the region we brought backgrounds that were new to this region for judicatory leaders. We both had experience in leading large entrepreneurial congregations, consulting with them, or attending their seminars. We both thought about congregations in terms of growth, health, complexity, and largeness. In fact our bias is toward congregations that are large and healthy rather than congregations that are small and dysfunctional. We also recognized that smallness and largeness are not the primary characteristic, because smaller congregations can be healthy, and larger ones are not necessarily healthy just because they are large. However, we did believe that static or declining congregations regardless of size are reflections of both spiritual and institutional dysfunction. We knew that small congregations that do not grow are unhealthy and large congregations that simply contribute to the rearranging of sheep by growing at the expense of smaller congregations are also unhealthy.

This large, healthy, congregational mindset is foundational to the changes we have experienced. In fact, I would argue that in the United States it should be seen as a foundational principle for change in judicatories. Since we came with this mindset, we acted out a strategy that was not stated intentionally but was implemented. We decided to run the judicatory the way a senior pastor runs a large, entrepreneurial congregation. This decision led to a very different strategic plan. For example, we thought in terms of what is best to accomplish the mission rather than preserve the institution. We were more concerned about developing effective strategies than in perpetuating meetings, events, and traditions that did not contribute to the mission. Leaders who were effective, successful, open to risk, willing to change, trying new paradigms, and willing to be held accountable for their ministries were honored over those who viewed themselves as "loyal soldiers" who had been carrying out denominational mandates for a number of years. We were willing to terminate inefficient and ineffective systems and programs and replace them with new strategies that worked and helped us accomplish the mission. We were open to changing the status quo and changing new strategies when they failed to work, thereby forcing us to create even newer ones. We were open to confronting individuals who were unable to make the changes or who even worked against the changes. We adopted and implemented new values that were required for change and discarded those that were hindering health and growth. Finally, our commitment to the mission and vision took precedence over everything including those specific denominational concerns that we felt hindered the accomplishment of the mission and achieving the vision.

This mindset committed us to the belief that any congregation, regardless of location, size, history, or context could become a large one. I still believe that this is true. If a congregation is spiritually on track with the heart of God, has the right leadership, and is willing to accept the cost, it can become healthy, effective, and large regardless of the circumstances. The two major problems facing any congregation are this: 1) willingness to put God's agenda above their own needs, and 2) the lack of leadership by both pastors and laity.

Large, healthy congregational thinking means that one leads by attraction, not compulsion. That is exactly what our judicatory needed. As Baptists, where congregations are autonomous and where judicatory leaders for the most part must lead through influence rather than command, such leadership thinking is required. However, I would argue that denominations that have much more leverage over pastors and congregations than in Baptist circles still must lead by attraction rather than command. Leading by command, even if you have the ability to do so, ignores the culture in which we live. People may obey you when they must, but they will not follow you anywhere. Therefore deep systemic change only comes, I believe, when you attract people to your significant mission and compelling vision to address a worthwhile need.

I do not believe that the executive judicatory leaders must be selected from pastors and key staff in large entrepreneurial congregations, although that might be an excellent way to choose them. However, judicatory leaders should be people who have led large entrepreneurial enterprises, whether it be in the Christian or non-Christian world. They need to be people who understand how to effectively lead a large, complex organization that is missional in nature, visionary in achievement, strategic in thinking, and willing to hold itself accountable to goals and results. They need to be people who understand the nature of deep systemic change and how to effectively lead people through that change.

Leading with Mission

The mission of an organization basically states the bottom-line purpose for which that particular organization exists. In dysfunctional and dying organizations the mission is usually maintaining the status quo of the organization, to keep it from dying. At the beginning of the intervention, our regional leaders adopted a new mission statement which was and continues to be: "The American Baptist Churches of the West exist to grow healthy churches." We mean it literally, and we began to produce alignment between our current or new institutional behaviors and this mission. You will notice that this mission statement caused us to focus on the local congregation as the primary unit of mission. Even though we were committed to our denominational identity, and in no way saw our-selves as leaving it or even trying to change it, our primary com-mitment was to the local congregations in our region, not the denomination. Preferably, such a commitment should not produce conflict between the judicatory and the national entity. However, when there are competing agendas for finances, publicity, time, and people, there are always conflicts. Our mission statement, if it has integrity, meant that when such conflicts arose, the local congrega-tion and its needs took priority.

We stopped promoting musical pulpits among pastors who want-ed to change locations every four or five years, whether their con-gregations had grown or not. We stopped rewarding regional staff members for maintaining the status quo. We stopped subsidizing our camps when they failed to run at a profit. We stopped triangu-lation by discouraging the use of pastoral relations committees. We stopped conflict mediation that usually resulted in the pastor leav-ing and the congregation remaining on a plateau or declining.

On the other hand, we began to introduce training for region staff consultants, pastors, and lay leaders. We rewarded region staff members and honored those pastors and congregations that were changing and growing. We gave new camp leaders the right to run their affairs without a lot of regional interference and watched them obliterate their red ink and make a profit. We trained pastors and boards to set specific, measurable, and behavioral goals, so a pas-toral relations committee was no longer needed. We watched as congregations grew. We replaced conflict mediation with congrega-tional consultations and saw change as congregations moved from spiritual and organization dysfunction to health.

Developing this alignment process brought a barrage of criticism since we were no longer doing things the way they had been done before. We were in a sense denying some ministries and behaviors that at one time had been quite productive but no longer were. This is one reason why being a leader takes courage, particularly in the Christian world where the abandonment of certain behaviors is personalized and often viewed as character rejection. However, if we had continued to do the same things we would have generated the same results we had been getting, which eventually would have led to a growing number of extinct congregations and eventually the death of the region.

Leading through Vision

When the region leaders adopted a mission that placed the focus of the region's efforts upon the local congregation as God's basic unit of mission, we believed that the mission was right and worth pursuing. However, we knew that a correct mission does not bring about change. Therefore, we needed to develop a vision of what it would look like if the mission was actually accomplished. We had to provide people an idea of a preferable future that was far better then the current state of affairs.

This vision needs to be big enough to stir the blood, specific enough to be accomplished, and short enough to be put on a bumper sticker. Our vision was that we would see at least seventy percent of our congregations growing at the end of five years. This vision was so big that most did not believe it could be achieved. In fact, many national denominational entities have over the past two decades of decline set forth similar bold visions, to knowing smiles of disbelief about the false bravado. But at the judicatory level, when reorganized along the lines described in this book, this objective and implications are exciting enough to catch the attention of the people in congregations. It also raised the level of accountability for those leading it because now there are specific times (January, 2002) and amounts (seventy-two percent of our congregations) tied to the accomplishment of the mission. We gave people an idea of what an accomplished mission would look like.

I personally believe that an exciting vision brings emotional fuel for change. It enables many, even if they are doubtful, to dream of a better outcome. It taps into our soul and says that things need not be as bad as they are today. I think vision is the biblical way of communicating hope to both individuals and groups of people. Our vision was seen as so big that if it were accomplished God had to be both behind it and in it.

There are several key strategies to leading through vision. The first is that the leader must communicate the vision often, at the risk of redundancy. Second, the vision must not be presented as an option to the status quo. The status quo must be presented as unacceptable, with the vision an excellent new option for a better and more effective way of living. Finally, the leader must believe enough in God and God's people to assume that the vision can be accomplished.

Every time we communicate to either individuals or groups we must be sharing some aspect of the vision. I know that I can take three hours and share my vision with anyone, giving the details, reasons, motivations, strategies, and tactics related to it. However, I can also communicate the overall vision in less than three minutes. I see my primary task as Executive Minister to be the keeper and caster of the vision and mission. My role when I preach, lead, administer, and train is to always do it so that it relates to the vision and mission. I constantly see myself as a persuader, helping individuals and groups understand, embrace, or implement our vision and therefore accomplish the mission God has given us.

There are a number of tactics related to the strategy of constantly communicating the vision. First, I need time and flexibility to be that kind of communicator. We have an excellent person who functions as our regional administrator. This individual deals with most the of the daily operations of the region, including taking most of the phone calls that come to us from pastors and congregational leaders. I am constantly amazed when I talk to other judicatory leaders who have similar positions at how much they are on the phone, particularly with pastors. They tell me of how they often deal with twenty to thirty calls a day. It is no wonder they do not have time to think, to plan, to strategize, and to communicate vision and mission. Visionary leaders must stay in touch with key people and pastors, but they cannot function as chaplains, problem solvers, or managers dealing with the day to day issues of region life.

A second tactic related to communicating vision is the use of story. I believe that vision is best communicated through the telling of stories. Stories are metaphors that elicit involvement. They not only communicate main ideas, they demonstrate how those ideas are lived out in real situations, while drawing listeners in to hearing how their peers have handled similar situations. I have come to realize as a congregational consultant that often my best persuasion tool to produce change is to share with one congregation how another congregation has dealt effectively with similar issues. Stories are vehicles of hope. Much of my task is sharing with congregations in one part of the region how others in another section of the region are progressing, changing, and seeing God bless their risk-taking. Therefore, I work at collecting stories, particularly those related to different groups. I use stories of effective pastors with pastors, stories of effective boards with boards, stories of effective assimilation leaders with those attempting to start assimilation ministries in their congregations. I also work at telling stories well, which sometimes means giving an abridged version, due to time or other constraints.

A third tactic I use in communicating vision is to make sure that when I preach or speak to groups I always ask the "so what" question of my idea in relation to what the entire group should believe, think, or do. Usually when we preach or speak we tell individuals what we think they should believe, think, or do but seldom do we make application to the group as a whole entity. However, speaking to the entire group and offering application to the group communicates vision. It enables the group to see what they can accomplish as a group. It enables individuals to find value in being part of something larger than themselves. Therefore, when I speak at regional events I discuss what "we" as a region should think, believe, or do. When speaking to a congregation I offer a number of applications to the entire congregation as a congregation.

A second strategy in leading through vision is painting the status quo as unacceptable rather than as an alternative to the vision. A good leader recognizes that she or he must help the group see that the current situation is untenable. If the group does nothing about its current situation it will get worse.

At the beginning of an intervention our job was to create legitimate emotional imbalance among the pastors, leaders, and congregations within the region, both about the congregations and the region itself. We wanted people to say, "enough is enough we will no longer tolerate the condition in which we find ourselves." However, once people reach that state, the next issue relates to what will be done to move from where they are to a preferable future. This is why with anecdote we always communicate the vision as the antidote to the status quo.

The vision we painted for our region was a large group of growing, healthy congregations filled with younger people and children, reaching their communities with the good news, that God loves them, and offers all people eternal life through Jesus Christ. We told congregations of sixty, 100, or 125 that they could be congregations of 300, 400, or even 700, filled with new life, youth, vitality, spiritual dynamics and having far more influence than they ever thought possible. We then helped them to see that as congregations grew in health, size, and effectiveness their budgets would also grow. These growing budgets would positively impact the ministries of the congregations, the region, the denomination, and other missions endeavors around the world.

In essence we painted a contrast. The choice was the eventual death of both congregations and the region, or a new life that would produce even greater ministry effectiveness than had ever been seen by congregations within the region. When viewed from that perspective the choice was not difficult. Living out the choice was, and continues to be, difficult and costly to personal comfort, but the initial choice was not a hard one to make for most pastors, leaders, and congregations.

Perhaps the biggest act of leadership that came from casting vision as a better option than remaining with the status quo was getting the congregations to free up half of the last reserves (two million dollars) over three years to spend for training and recruitment. Approximately two million of the four million remaining dollars had been designated in some way and could not be touched. This left two million dollars as savings, which was invested so that the interest supported the region's general budget. We made a proposal to our constituents, the congregations, that we take that remaining two million dollars and invest it in two major areas over a three-year period. The first area was that of training. The money was used to expose scholarship pastors and lay persons to the best trainers in the country.

The second area of investment went toward attracting pastors of growing congregations in other parts of the country to come here and lead congregations when openings arose. We needed to raise the caliber of expectations for pastors, and the best way to do that was to attract those who already understood the basic concepts of congregational health and growth. However, we understood that we needed added financial resources to develop this particular strategy, and if the congregations voted to free this money up, it would be used for this purpose. We now believe that these funds were a grand and worthwhile investment that enabled us to do what we needed to provide the turn around. We have also calculated that in the last six years since this decision was made, we have been able to generate between 1.2 and 1.5 million new missions dollars that would have never been available if we had not made this decision.

Leading with New Values

Many people today talk about mission and vision as necessary for both change and effective ministry. Why then do we develop new missions and cast new visions but so often see nothing happen that produces either change or effectiveness? I believe that when this occurs it is because people have failed to understand that the values of the organization must be changed at the same time. By values I mean the basic beliefs that are embedded within people in the organization, some of which they do not even know they possess. In fact often if you ask people to articulate those values they seldom can. Therefore, you discover what a group's values are by looking at their behavior; how they spend money, how they treat people, what they do most consistently, what they fail to do unless forced. The values are best seen when the group faces some kind of stress, and you then see how people within the group behave and make decisions.

When new missions are adopted and new visions are cast, you must also change basic core values. The changing of such values assumes that you will discard those that run counter to the new mission and vision, while adopting those that are consistent with them.

One example of a value to discard is the shepherd role of the pastor (described in Chapter 1), which means that most of the time, energy, and resources of the region were spent on the congregations that were the smallest, the most conflicted and troubled, and produced the least amount of missions dollars, rather than on the congregations that were doing the best job of demonstrating health and growth.

Therefore, we needed to develop some strategies to address the issue of changing values. The first strategy related to the visionary task of making people uncomfortable with the status quo as we cast the new vision. The second strategy was simply the changing of behaviors to reflect new values. The third strategy was to share stories of how the implementation of new values produced new behaviors, which in turn produced health, growth, and effective ministry.

Part of helping people become dissatisfied with the status quo is demonstrating to them how current thinking has led to the present condition. We began to talk constantly about leadership. We shared what leadership was, what it demanded, and the benefits of being an effective leader. We also demonstrated that functioning on a chaplain model where the primary goals are caring for people and helping maintain harmony among the sheep is quite limiting in terms of the number of people that can be ministered to by one person. We also demonstrated that such mentality drives away others who are not attracted by this model, thus leaving the group often ministering to only very needy and co-dependent people. We tried to help people see that many of their congregations as well as the region were in a whirlpool of behavior that kept sucking more and more resources into the depths, with nothing productive happening. At the same time we demonstrated that a leadership model could still meet the needs of individuals (as leaders equipped the saints for the work of ministry) while accomplishing much more.

Along with other consultants I was confrontational with pastors and congregational leaders about Jesus' mandate to go and make disciples. I pointed out that this was not happening in our congregations and as a result we were being disobedient and failing to meet the very purpose for the church's existence. I then tried to show the values, and in turn behaviors, that had led to this predicament. Through the consultation process we then offered a better way of acting which would demand a change in values for the congregation.

A second strategy was to simply change behaviors. Our first action was to tell our current pastors that we would not help them find another position in the region if the congregation they were leaving was not growing. We wanted to demonstrate that leaders must be held accountable for leading. Leadership and all that it entailed was a new value we wanted pastors to embrace.

A second action we stopped was conducting conflict mediation. We really believed that conflict mediation in congregations for the most part does not work, only produces more conflict mediation, never produces organizational health or growth, and communicates that most of the region's resources need to be focused on the islands of sickness rather than on islands of health.

Conflict mediation does not produce healthy congregations, since it is focused on conflict within the congregation rather than control of the congregation. Conflict mediation assumes that the fighting parties will come to the process with some degree of integrity. In dysfunctional congregations the lack of spirituality inhibits people from possessing such integrity, plus the mediators are seeking resolution in what is already a dysfunctional situation. When the real issue of conflict is the control of the congregation (this issue is never the stated issue), those with the control will never give it up unless forced to do so. The nature and purpose of conflict mediation is to get believers to be reconciled, not deal with the control issues that cause congregations to remain dysfunctional. Also, since most conflict mediators do not truly understand the missional responsibility of biblical congregations, or have a deep commitment to moving the congregation from dysfunction to health, they mediate in areas that produce no real substantive change for the congregation as a whole. Third, for a congregation to move from dysfunction to health, it usually requires that those in control now can no longer have any say in the direction of the congregation. Yet these people usually perceive themselves to be either the most biblically literate or the most spiritually wise individuals in the congregation, which is why they think they should be in control. After all they usually have hung around the longest, investing the most time and sometimes the most money in the life of the congregation. The removal of these people of influence will not occur through mediation. Often it takes intervention or confrontation. Agriculturalists understand that growing grass means focusing on the growth of the lawn, not the destruction of weeds. Conflict mediation focuses on the removal of weeds.

A third behavior we stopped was the honoring of those who were loyal and faithful but unfruitful. Obviously, faithfulness and loyalty are good virtues. However, these two attributes must always be dealt with in context. Faithfulness is important and valued if the faithfulness is producing fruit. Faithfulness without fruit is epitomized by the steward who hid his talent in the ground. The steward was faithful in keeping the talent but was judged by the master for the lack of fruit. The talent was his stewardship to invest and risk, not guard.

Loyalty is important and valuable if people are loyal to the right cause. Also, a loyalty that is not critical of that to which the person is being loyal may be a human value but it surely is not a spiritual one. If my child commits murder, I will still love and support my child while recognizing that my loyalty to my child does not interfere with the legal system that seeks to bring justice to the situation. Today we honor an individual like Dietrich Bonhoeffer, whose loyalty to God caused him to break even relations with other clergy and his national leaders. Therefore we began to honor those pastors and congregations that were open to change, that took leadership seriously, that wanted to be held accountable to fulfilling the Great Commission, and that were committed to helping other congregations do the same. Currently we have eighteen congregations in our region that average over 500 in worship attendance. Fifteen of the pastors of those congregations support the mission of the region through missions dollars, time, opening facilities for training, etc. The reason is that we have honored them, along with a good number of other pastors whose congregations are growing. In doing so we have not honored those pastors and congregations that are unwilling to take the Great Commission seriously and be held accountable to it.

The third strategy we employed to lead individuals and congregations to adopt new values was through the use of story. The Executive Minister and I had many stories from congregations we had led, consulted, and observed. We could provide specific examples of behaviors that reflected different values than those currently being embraced in the region. We also had many tragic stories of congregations that failed to embrace new values and behave differently and as a result faced hard consequences.

However, part of the reason for bringing in well-known leaders to provide training was to expose our leaders and congregations to people who lived and practiced values we needed to adopt. As they told their stories and demonstrated the changes they made it re-enforced what we were saying. They became the experts because they were coming from a distance, plus it was obvious from their ministries that what they were saying was true.

The new mission and vision gained momentum as the new values were adopted. They actually fed upon each other. We needed to turn the whirlpool of discouragement around and that took hard work. But as we progressed the water began to turn more easily in a new direction. This is why good leaders understand that old values must be discarded and new values adopted in order for a new mission and vision to succeed.

Leadership and Structure

Each of the changes we instituted related to mission, vision, values, and now structure, are based upon bedrock beliefs. These beliefs are core to the behaviors we introduced into the region and into congregations. They are fundamental to all we did and are doing today as a judicatory. These beliefs are so crucial that they are discussed as the last chapter of this book.

The structure of the region would not allow a new mission to be implemented or a new vision to be accomplished. The region was a well-oiled bureaucracy that had many people performing many good tasks that were not producing effective congregations. There were over fifty people on the region's board. There were a large number of committees and commissions that met regularly to discuss different ministry issues and create policies. An extensive number of policy manuals, related to a variety of operating procedures and behaviors had been created. Yet all of this activity that occurred throughout the year at great expense and a greater cost in time was not resulting in growing healthy congregations. In fact the opposite was occurring, congregations were dying, and so was the region.

There were several key values that produced this behavior. One was the belief that many people needed to have their say on a number of matters, whether they were equipped or qualified to speak. Second, one way of practicing control so no one would have too much authority was to separate authority from responsibility. Also, committees were a way for people to hold power without anyone being held accountable for results.

We knew that as we led people to become dissatisfied with the status quo and in turn embrace the vision there would be a lot of initial excitement. However, once the actual work of changing behaviors and exposing poor values was in process many would want to slow down or stop the process altogether. We also knew that if we had to spend time keeping the machinery of the bureaucracy going we would not have the time to create, develop, and implement new strategies and tactics.

Therefore, we adopted another foundational principle: Eliminate the structure that inhibits the implementation of the mission and vision. We employed several strategies to implement the principle.

First, we attacked this issue in describing the status quo as unacceptable and offered a vision of what could be if the structure was different. Second, we offered an alternative that we felt would be acceptable to the leaders of the region, who would probably resist a new structure.

We began to point out to people that all the effort, time, and money in keeping the machinery going simply was not working. This did not require too much convincing with people who had served on committees and commissions and wondered what they were doing there, what was being accomplished, or why they were even needed. It did take more convincing for those longtime participants who had not realized that judicatory work had become their fellowship network. In fact the smaller and more dysfunctional their congregations had become, the more they looked forward to regional work because of the friends they had made, with resulting relationships that were meaningful to them.

Therefore, we, the regional leaders went to the constituents, the congregations, and said that the region should try a grand experiment. We delineated the parts of our by-laws that related to the month-by-month operating of the region that interfered with new strategies and tactics of ministry being implemented. We told our constituents that we would like their vote to place these parts of our by-laws in abeyance for three years while new ways of functioning were developed. A new structure would then be presented to the constituents at the end of three years. At that time they could vote on whether to adopt the new structure or return to the old one.

This strategy did a number of things. First, it enabled the congregations to allow change knowing that if it did not work they could go back to the old way of doing business. Second, it held us, the leadership of the region, accountable to lead others to accept the mission and embrace the vision in such a way that the new structure would be accepted. The vote on the structure in three years would be a confirmation or rejection of the new mission and vision. It would also reflect whether the new values were truly beginning to become imbedded or not.

Three years later the new structure, reflecting the new ways of operating, was adopted by a two-thirds vote of the region's constituents. At this point the informal structure became formalized. The congregations in a real sense voted their approval of the new mission and vision.

All of this came about, from a human perspective, because new leaders were leading by mission, vision, values, and structure. We understood that systemic change does not occur if these four foundational issues are not implemented successfully. We also understood that they all work together and I believe that if one of the four is missing you do not see long-term systemic change.

New Leadership for Judicatories

Strong judicatory leaders in the twenty-first century must be people who have a passion for God and the Great Commission, for it is out of such passion that one derives courage. If I believe I am on a mission given by God, that is, the correct biblical mission, then I am willing to take the slings and arrows that come with leading change. I may not like the criticism, but I can withstand it if I realize that I am leading the right mission and doing the right things.

I must be willing to communicate the mission and vision to a level of redundancy. I must be clear about the overall strategies while recognizing that specific details will constantly change. In fact, I must be willing to fail, for without experimentation there will not be success. However, in the midst of all the activity I must keep communicating mission and vision, encouraging people to follow God and be a part of something big and grand that only God can do.

Leadership is the key to change. When judicatories select the right leaders and let them lead, God can, I believe, do awesome things.

Chapter Four
Restoring the Congregation to its Rightful Place

A PIECE OF OUR STORY

A congregation in our region at one time had over 500 people attending worship services. When I came the congregation had approximately 120 in worship in a setting that would hold over three hundred. The congregation was aging. There were less than five children under the age of five and only a handful of teenagers involved in any way. The current pastor had been there for ten years during which time the congregation had declined. The leaders, including the pastor, told me they were ready for change, needed to grow, and did not want to die.

This congregation was one of the first congregations I selected for intense work. I led the people through a congregational consultation. We helped them develop an outward-focused mission and vision. I helped them restructure so that the pastor was the leader and the board began to govern. Through this process the current pastor left. I then assisted the congregation in finding a new pastor who was a strong leader, an evangelist, with a track record of turning around dysfunctional congregations.

When the new pastor came on board everyone was excited. In his first year the congregation grew to almost two hundred, much of it a result of new people entering into a relationship with Jesus Christ. At that point a number of long-term members began to resist the new pastor's leadership and the changes underway. Their resistance grew to the point of sending letters, calling people, and using congregational meetings to voice their displeasure. As the resistance grew many of the new people began to leave and the congregation's numbers began to decline.

During this time I saw my responsibility to offer help and hope to the pastor, the board, and those members of the congregation who still wanted health and growth. Some of those resisting had contact with our national leaders, who did nothing to help the pastor or congregation. I

also saw my role as protecting the pastor and leaders from any undue denominational pressure.

Eventually those who were dissenting to the changes were asked to leave the congregation. Many others joined them in leaving. These people created their own Web site, came to regional meetings wearing signs expressing their dissatisfaction, and continued to share their feelings with people in the congregation, region, and denomination.

However, once that particular group left, the congregation began to grow again. In 2003 the congregation is once again averaging close to five hundred in worship. Much of the growth has come through reaching unchurched people who have had no previous personal relationship with God or Jesus Christ. The main newspaper in the area reported that this congregation is the only mainline Protestant congregation in the county that is growing rather than declining.

I believe that these results are due in part to the region focusing on the local congregation as God's major unit of mission. We have poured our resources into this congregation. We have also protected the pastor and leaders from those in the congregation, the region, and the denomination who wanted to stop the changes.

When judicatories are serious about recognizing congregations as the primary unit of mission, it means that the congregations then become the primary customer of regional focus, attention, and resources. It means that the most important people in regional life are the pastors and lay leaders of congregations. The region exists to serve these leaders first, before considering any demands that go with being part of a larger denominational entity. In essence the top of the denominational hierarchy is the local congregation and the most important people in the denomination are the pastors and lay leaders of the congregations. This upside-down way of looking at denominations means that regional leaders come next in this new hierarchy, since they are closest to the congregations, with national leaders being at the bottom of the structure. Perhaps this is why it is better to see the relationships in regard to the archery metaphor used in Chapter 1, with the local congregation being the bullseye of the target.

The above relationships are crucial to the turn-around process in congregations. Many older denominationally related parishioners hold the judicatory and denomination with a respect that is both healthy and unhealthy. The respect is healthy in supporting effective ministries that are led by either denominations or judicatories. This respect is unhealthy in that often the current ineptness of modern denominational and judicatory life is not criticized or challenged, since it is simply our denominational "family." We used this respect to help produce congregational change.

As local congregational leaders began to risk in leading their respective congregations from dysfunction to health, those resisting the change often contacted judicatory leaders. It was at this point we assured these resisters that their congregational leaders were on track and needed their support even when the change produced deep pain. For some of the critics our support was enough. When that occurred the change happened more quickly, because the judicatory had thrown its support and credibility behind congregational leaders. Other congregational critics however, were frustrated with our support of their leaders. They in turn went around the judicatory and complained to national leaders. These national leaders by and large did not support the leaders at either the congregational level or the regional level. When this occurred the change process was slowed down considerably. These critics created havoc with members of the congregation by playing their denomination's leaders against each other. Their actions were much like a child playing parents against each other so the child does not have to do her or his homework.

Several strategies can be used to emphasize that the congregation is the primary reason for the existence of a judicatory.

The first strategy is to treat each congregation as its own micro-culture. By this I mean that there is no one magic fix that can help each congregation move from dysfunction to health. The primary tactic we used to work with congregations was a congregational consultation. However, in every consultation we treated each congregation as a unique entity that needed to implement systemic changes in ways that were best for that congregation and would only work with that congregation.

There are a variety of factors that make congregations unique. However, in order to summarize these different factors I refer to two simple categories. These categories are external factors, meaning those things outside the congregation that make it unique, and internal factors, those things within a congregation that make it different from all others.

External factors include the size of the community, its culture and history, its economics, its age. For example, we had one highly dysfunctional congregation that turned around that was predominately comprised of younger families, children, and teenagers. This congregation was located in a true bedroom community. Living in that community meant that you went to other communities to shop, attend movies, eat at restaurants, or have other cultural experiences. People from other communities did not visit this community even to attend church. The community, for the most part, had more younger people living in it than older folk. As a result, the congregation, though on a plateau and controlled by a few people who restricted growth, was much younger in average age than many of our other dysfunctional congregations.

Internal factors relate to such things as the congregation's history, values, beliefs, self-image, and perceived strengths and weaknesses. For example, we had a congregation that eventually closed, which had first formed when a larger congregation left our denomination. The people started this congregation, which lasted less than twenty-five years, as a response to the bigger congregation leaving the American Baptist family. The congregation's identity was defined by this event. One of the highlights in this congregation's short history was how this small congregation's softball team had once beaten the team from their former larger congregation. The win had come by forfeit. This congregation could never get away from the negative vision that had led to its creation.

The second strategy was to use our region's influence to protect those congregations and congregational leaders that were taking the risk to change. We wanted them to know that they were not in this process alone and that we were not only asking congregations to change but were willing to risk with them in helping lead change.

The third strategy we used was to work at creating an atmosphere of interdependence and cooperation between pastors and congregations. We were convinced that both the region and our congregations would be much more effective in fulfilling the Great Commission if we could change a competitive mentality among pastors and leaders to a cooperative one. Autonomy does not mean independence. The New Testament writers were constantly encouraging congregations to work together, to pray for one another, and to aid one another.

Turning the Region Around One Congregation at a Time

As stated previously, each area consultant was to select seven to ten congregations in that consultant's area to work with intensively for a year. The consultant was to select those congregations believed to have the best chance of turning around. Sometime this choice was based on the current history of the congregation while other times it might be related to the intense desire for change expressed by the leaders. There was no one criterion used to select congregations. However, congregations were avoided if they were resistant to the new direction the region was taking, resistant to change, did not think they needed to change, or had pastors who were too threatened to discuss change. After all, we could only work with those congregations that invited us to do so. We did include growing congregations, of which there were only a few, because most that were growing were not experiencing growth because they were necessarily healthy but for other reasons.

Once these congregations were selected, by whatever process, we informed them that they would have to go through a congregational consultation. They were told it would take them several months to prepare for the consultation and that once it was over we would work with them for a year to implement the systemic changes required to help them move from dysfunction to taking steps to spiritual and organizational health.

It did not take long to learn that consulting with congregations is like getting a physical from a physician. The basic issues and systems related to health and disease are common to all human beings. Normally, if a people live a certain way they will experience more health or disease than if they live in a different way. However, every patient wants to be treated as an individual, and each individual responds in some unique ways to medical prescriptions or procedures. The same is true of congregations. There are basic issues related to spiritual health or spiritual dysfunction. In some ways many congregations are not hard to diagnose. Yet each congregation is quite unique.

This uniqueness is first determined by the people the congregation comprises. They are all different personalities, with different gifting, possessing peculiar features in how they look at God, their congregation, and their personal mission within a congregation. Second, each congregation is unique in regard to its history. No congregation resides in a time vacuum. Most congregational pathologies, both positive and negative are rooted in the near or distant history of the congregation. Third, each congregation is called to reach a particular community and in many cases a particular niche within a community. Just as Jesus Christ has put a variety of members in one local body, God has often put a variety of bodies in one local community. Fourth, each congregation carries out its mission and vision with special nuances unique to that individual congregation.

Therefore, in consulting with congregations we had to deal with issues that are endemic to all congregations while at the same time helping each congregation work through the implementation of its mission and vision in ways that were unique to that congregation. Flexibility is a foundational principle underlying our strategy of treating each congregation as a microculture.

Each dysfunctional congregation has a number of basic elements that need to be changed. However, how that congregation arrived at where it is today, what is required to change and who will lead that change, and how they will implement their new mission and vision is quite unique. During a consultation we could not make many assumptions going into the consultation about how the process was going to work itself out.

We also refrained from suggesting any universal philosophy of ministry for a congregation to follow as a result of the consultation. Each congregation was free to select that philosophy of ministry that best fit them and their leaders. Since we had encouraged many leaders to learn from the models of ministry implemented at Saddle Back and Willow Creek, many thought we were leading congregations to accept a seeker-driven model. That simply was not the case, although we urged our congregations to be seeker-friendly and sensitive in the manner in which they conducted corporate ministry. In fact, we went the opposite way, suggesting that they not adopt a seeker-driven model since we believed that leading established congregations into such a model would be counter-productive to change and organizational health. I believed that this change was so drastic that it would inhibit the congregation's ability to move from dysfunction to health.

Tools for Conducting Congregational Consultations

The most foundational principle in conducting a congregational consultation is getting information about the congregation. The more information a consultant has, the more effective the consultation. We used two major tools to obtain this information. One tool, a self-study, was given to every congregation with whom we consulted. The second tool, a survey, was used with congregations that had one hundred or more adults in worship attendance.

In 1994 Leith Anderson and I obtained a grant from Leadership Network to create a new organization called Teaching Church Network. The purpose of Teaching Church Network was to enlist larger effective congregations to enter into mentoring relationships with smaller congregations that wanted to increase the effectiveness of their ministry. During the period from 1994 to 1997 I conducted Wooddale's congregational mentoring program, which provided a mentoring pattern that many of our Teaching Churches followed. Part of Wooddale's mentoring program required congregations to conduct a self-study. When I came to ABCW I used this self-study document with our congregations. Since that time it has gone through a number of changes.

The primary purpose of the self-study is to get the leaders of a congregation to provide the consultant with information about the congregation prior to the consultant's visit. If the document is followed well and the answers provided are accurate, complete without being verbose, and processed well by the congregational leaders, the consultant usually has more than enough information to conduct a thorough consultation. Also, if the leaders do not follow the process well and provide information that is off target or incomplete, a good consultant is able to learn much about that congregation by what is not done or done poorly.

The second purpose of the self-study was to create a positive emotional investment in the consulting process with the leaders of the congregation. Generally, we asked the main board of the congregation, if the congregation had more than one, to oversee the self-study process. We told them that this process would be quite beneficial to the consultant while at the same time giving them information about the congregation that would be helpful to them. We also told them that this process, while costing them time, did not cost them money. As they either performed the study themselves or assigned others to gather information for them, they began to have an investment in the process. We knew the more they invested their time and energy the more committed they would probably be to carrying out prescriptions once the actual consultation was completed.

The self-study, which usually took a congregation two or three months to complete, asked for information relating to eight major areas, as follows:

1. Congregational History, Congregational Personnel, and the Community

2. Congregation's Purpose, Goals, and Programs

3. Congregational Governance, Staffing, Structure, and Beliefs

4. Basic Demographic Information and Numerical Records

5. Financial and Stewardship Information

6. Focus Group Results—Conducted by Leaders

7. Documents and Materials in Print

8. Evaluation by Those Leading the Self-Study Process

The congregation was asked to get all of this information to the consultant at least two weeks prior to the scheduled consultation.

I had trained our consultants to read all this information with an eye to seeing what was being said, and to look at what was not being said. I told our consultants that the self-study material should generate for them fifty to 100 questions, many of which would be asked either prior to the consultation or during it. I also told them that they should call the pastor, if one was in place, and if not call a key staff person or lay leader, before the consultation, to pursue any major issues raised by the self-study information.

It is important to state at this juncture that we always went into the consultation supporting the pastor and attempting to conduct the consultation to prepare the pastor to be the primary leader of change. I knew that we were doomed from the start if these consultations were ever perceived as ways to help congregations get rid of pastors. In our congregations at least, pastors are the gatekeepers that either let you in to consult, make the consultation process easy or difficult, or stop it altogether. Therefore, I wanted our consultants to keep our pastors informed during the process, ask any embarrassing questions in private, and be alerted to potential problems that might deeply affect the pastor's leadership of that congregation.

The second tool we used was the Church Development Survey produced by the Institute for Church Development in Denver Colorado.[1] This survey has been used with approximately 1,000 congregations representing a quarter-million participants. I began to use this survey when I taught at Denver Seminary, which at that time owned it. The purpose of the survey is to help a congregation develop a spiritual demography of its overall ministry. The survey reveals whether a congregation's individual ministries as well as its overall ministry are being conducted effectively or ineffectively. One advantage of this survey is that enough congregations around the country have taken it that any congregation can compare its results against the survey's database and get a good measure for how well they are doing in individual areas of ministry, as well as its overall ministry effectiveness.

I prefer the tools that I used because I am familiar with them and believe they helped me generate the information that I need. However, I am not convinced that the tools are the real key. I believe there are many other excellent surveys and assessment tools available to consultants. The key is generating as much accurate information as possible about a congregation in preparing for a consultation.

The Process of Conducting Congregational Consultations

The normal process for conducting a congregational consultation was to select a weekend during which the entire focus of the congregation would be related to the consultation. Obviously schedules and formats varied, but I will describe a typical consultation weekend for congregations of less than 200 in worship attendance where there was usually only one full-time ministerial staff person, the pastor.

The consultant would begin to interview the pastor on Friday afternoon, with the interview continuing through dinner. We wanted the pastor's spouse at dinner with no children around so the spouse could participate fully in her or his part of the interview. This interview was designed to accomplish a number of things. One was to provide answers for the many questions generated by the consultant while the data was being gathered. Two, we wanted to determine the pastor and spouse's commitment to remain with that congregation and work through changes. Third, we wanted the pastor to help us understand what we would encounter during the consultation weekend and who would be the most resistant to change and why that was so. Fourth, we wanted to know how we could help the pastor deal with those people most resistant to change. Fifth, we wanted to know if there was anything too sensitive to be dealt with in public forums that still needed the consultant's attention. And sixth, we wanted to know from the pastor's perspective what were his or her hopes, fears, aspirations, concerns about the weekend and the entire consultation process.

On Friday evening we asked the pastor to put together a focus group of twenty to twenty-five individuals who represented a cross-section of the congregation in age, backgrounds, length of time in attendance, and so forth. The only people we did not want in this group were leaders, including the pastor, for two reasons: The leaders would be given other opportunities to talk, and we wanted those in the focus group to feel free to share their views.

We always asked the focus group three questions: 1) What is it that you like about this congregation? 2) What is it that you would change about this congregation to make it better? 3) Assuming that getting enough people and money are not problems, what would you like to see this congregation accomplishing in the next five years? If there was time we would then ask questions about major issues that were surfacing as the data was being accumulated. We also always asked people, who were relatively new to the congregation, about how easy or difficult it was to become a part of this group.

We spent six hours with the leaders on Saturday, from 9:00 AM to 3:00 PM, including the pastor and board. If the pastor and board were comfortable with having other key leaders there, they were invited as well. First, time was set aside for interviewing the board about key issues that had arisen in the data or had surfaced during the interview with the pastor or in the focus group. Second, we gave them our interpretation of all the data we had collected to that point. Usually we summarized the data by sharing with them the top strengths and weaknesses (*concerns* is the term we used) facing the congregation. It was at this point that we pulled no punches and were completely honest. For example, if the congregation was headed for closure we often laid out a timeline of what that might look like. Third, we began to teach the leaders about what it took to have a healthy congregation. We ended the time with a list of specific prescriptions, usually listed in priority order, that we felt were mandatory to begin to move from spiritual and organizational dysfunction to health. It was at this point we wanted to offer hope that in most cases a turnaround was possible.

On Sunday morning the best preacher among the consultants preached a message of hope and vision, encouraging the congregation to embrace change. The rest of the consulting team members were observing everything from the nursery to the parking lot. They were also informally interviewing people through their conversations, gathering even more data for the consultation.

Following the Sunday morning service the congregation served some kind of a meal, usually a covered dish or potluck affair. After that we gathered the congregation together for a town meeting. The agenda of this meeting was similar to that with the leaders, only done in an abbreviated fashion. We wanted the congregation to hear what was promising and disappointing about their situation. Also, we wanted them to learn that they needed to change and act differently in order to once again become effective in fulfilling their mission. We shared with them prescriptions so they too would know what would be required. We often ended this meeting with a challenge. That challenge was to embrace change and be renewed or to remain the same and die. We told them that such a choice is usually easy to make but quite difficult to implement. Therefore, they through their leaders needed to make some important decisions.

After the weekend consultation was completed the area consultant then presented a plan to the pastor and in some cases the board to determine how each month the consultant would work to begin implementing the prescriptions. Often I would attend monthly board meetings, acting as a consultant, facilitator, and sometimes a prophet holding people accountable for what they said they would do to change. Sometimes I would offer leadership training, training in developing specific ministries such as initiating small groups or developing an assimilation program, or board training to teach board members new responsibilities while helping them curtail behaviors that inhibited change.

I believe that one of the biggest contributors to the large number of congregations turning around was the ongoing contact for a year after the consultation weekend. The weekend functioned as a line in the sand, helping leaders and the congregation make the decision to change. The month-to-month contact enabled both leaders and the congregation to see what was required for change, and the consultant often functioned as a "parent," holding children responsible and accountable for changing.

Using Congregational Consultations as a Tool for Change

Many of our congregational consultations became a chance to start over and begin to function in a far more effective and healthy way. We encountered five foundational issues of change if a dysfunctional congregation is going to have any chance of moving toward spiritual and organizational health.

First, there are qualitative and quantitative differences between congregations that have broken the 200 attendance barrier and those that have not. Though there are other numerical barriers, the most fundamental is the 200 barrier. Most people tend to look at the quantitative difference without realizing that the qualitative one is radical, like the difference between a dog and a cat, an apple and an orange, a boy and a girl. For congregations it is the difference between small- and large-congregational behavior and thinking.

Therefore, when we consulted with any congregation of less than 200, even those with fifty or seventy in attendance we told them that they must begin to act and think like a congregation of 1,000. Thus, the congregation must first understand that their primary reason for existence was not to serve themselves. The leaders needed to help the people learn that they, the people of the congregation, were first and foremost on a mission from God. This mission was to reach people who do not know God or have a relationship with Jesus and help those people become disciples of Jesus. This mission must take priority over the self-interests of the congregation.

Second, the people were not to perceive themselves as a body that was friendly but rather as a place where people could make friends. Generally people become Jesus' disciples through relationships with people who are already his disciples. This means that a healthy, growing congregation is always forming new groups so that new people can develop new relationships with disciples already in the congregation.

Third, the board needed to give up control of leading the congregation to the pastor and the pastor's staff members. The pastors and staff members had to give up the control of the ministry to the laity of the congregation. This meant that the congregation needed to be led by staff members who saw their jobs as developing lay people to be disciples and leaders of ministries. Staff members were to equip people for the work of ministry rather than conducting the ministry themselves. The pastor and staff members were to be leaders who developed leaders, who in turn developed more leaders.

We told pastors and congregations that if they wanted to grow they must now begin to act the size they wanted to become. As of yet we have no congregations of 150 or less that have grown to 1,000, but we do have several such congregations that have grown from 300 to 700 in average worship attendance.

Second, we described mission as the bottom-line reason for a congregation's existence. We suggested to congregations that there are only three reasons for a congregation to exist: 1) They exist for the people who are already apart of the congregation, which gives them an inward focus. I believe this is the bottom-line mission for most congregations in the United States, regardless of what they say their mission is on paper. It is also why most congregations are small, declining, and dysfunctional in fulfilling any biblical reason for being. 2) They exist to minister to people who are not yet a part of the congregation. This produces an outward focus in a congregation. Most congregations do not exist for this purpose and most that do pursue this mission well because it was theirs from the birth of the congregation. 3) They exist to fulfill both of the previous two purposes. Congregations exist for both themselves and those who are not there yet. These congregations have both an inward and an outward focus.

In the consultation process we urged our congregations to adopt the third purpose. We did this because we did not believe that inwardly focused congregations could make the giant leap to becoming totally outwardly focused. However, we did tell our congregations that if they adopted the dual purpose they are faced with another issue immediately. That issue is determining which purpose takes priority. We told them that if the inward purpose took priority there was no reason to change. If however, the outward focus took priority, which meant that the people not yet part of the congregation were served first, the congregation would grow. We never told congregations to write mission statements. Instead we asked them to honestly answer the question about whether they had an outward or inward focus. I believe that an outward focus is the primary cause of a turnaround for any congregation.

Every congregation has the same mission, to fulfill the Great Commission. If a Christian congregation fails in that mission, there is no reason to exist. We even went so far as to tell congregations that the Great Commission and the Great Commandment are not equal in relation to purpose. First, if you understand the Great Commandment correctly you make the Great Commission a priority. Second, when congregations say they do both equally, usually meaning they focus on reaching out to those not yet a part of them and focus as well on meeting the needs of those already a part of the congregation, they never actually do both. Instead, over time the inward focus of meeting their own needs takes priority over the focus of reaching out to others not yet there. When a congregation states it has two equal purposes, it will usually gravitate to the one that is easiest to achieve and as a result turn inward.

Third, we described vision as what it would look like specifically in five years if the mission were accomplished. We asked congregations to think in terms of the number of people attending, the number of new baptisms that would be happening every year, the number of new ministries initiated. But most important, we asked people to think of what impact a new mission would have on their community. We wanted them to envision how the community would be changed through the ministry of a healthy growing congregation.

I challenged congregations to state their vision in terms of a changed community. I believe people want to be part of something bigger themselves and they want their congregation to accomplish ministry that is bigger than itself. Too often congregations write selfish visions that simply state what will happen to them. This action eventually leads a congregation back to an inward focus. Instead we wanted congregations to think of themselves as entities that would become meaningful and crucial in the fabric of their communities. It is this kind of thinking that stirs the blood and produces passion within a congregation. It is this kind of vision that attracts people to want both to be a part of such a congregation and serve sacrificially.

Fourth, we explained values as those core beliefs that congregations have of which they are not often even aware. They sometimes are "gut feelings" that people cling to and just know they are right, whether they represent truth or not. Often it was the current values that had led the congregation to turn inward and become dysfunctional. For example, the value of family had overtaken the value of mission. This is illustrated when good people leading worship faithfully and with strong commitments are inept. Yet because they are members who have strong relationships throughout the congregation, no one confronts them about how their lack of musical talent is driving away potential disciples. The congregation believes that maintaining harmony and keeping family ties intact is more important than reaching new people with the good news of eternal life. This value also reflects an inward focus where the congregation is operated more for those who are already a part of it than those who are yet to come.

The problem with addressing congregational values is that it is almost impossible to get people to share their real values, collectively or individually, since often they are not even aware of what they are. Instead people give you the "Sunday School" responses when talking about their values, meaning the correct biblical answers even if those answers are nowhere near correct for that particular congregation. You begin to learn about a congregation's true values when you observe their behavior, particularly under stress. In the consultation process the primary way of learning about values was to see how a congregation handled and distributed its funds. Jesus was quite correct when he stated that our hearts are very closely connected to our treasures. Congregations are no different. Another way of examining current values is to observe a congregation's behavior over time. That is why we requested an analytical history relating to those times of growth or decline in the congregation. However, these investigations and others did not help us begin to change a congregation's values in order to align them with a new outwardly focused mission and vision. This had to be accomplished another way.

The best way to expose poor values and give congregations the opportunity to embrace new values is to create stress. Therefore, in our prescription process we usually offered some ways to put the body under stress.

Keep in mind that before we created stress we worked with congregations on mission and vision. We then moved to values and structure. Our desire for more rapid change was the reason we dealt with these issues in this order.

The fifth issue that is crucial to producing fundamental change in dysfunctional congregations is to create a new structure that is aligned with the new outward focused mission and vision. To do this, you need to do something with the current structure that has contributed to and supports the current state of plateau and decline. In many cases we encouraged congregations to follow the example of the region and take those by-laws that related to the monthly operation of the congregation's ministries and vote to put them in abeyance for three years. In their place we suggested a structure that reflected a large congregation's mentality. We found that by touching structure we created stress, because the changes affected those who, often for years, had been in power, protected turf, and controlled the money and in turn the overall ministry of the congregation. This move exposed those who desired a congregation that was truly interested in reaching out to people versus those who wanted to control things, even if it meant that such control would bring eventual death to the congregation.

The creation of the new structure was our attempt to change two major issues that keep congregations small and lead to an inward focus and eventually death. First, most congregations separate authority from responsibility while holding no one accountable. For example, it is not uncommon for congregations to hire a youth pastor and give this person the responsibility for ministry while keeping the authority for the youth ministry in a youth committee. This means that the youth pastor must continually go to the youth committee for permission and dollars to carry out youth responsibilities. The committee can never be held accountable since that is the very nature of committees. We wanted to create a structure that married authority, responsibility, and accountability. We did this by creating staff-led congregations, regardless of size.

Second, we turned right side up the biblical model of congregational ministry. This meant that leaders were not hired to do the ministry. Instead they were employed to lead the congregation and equip the saints to do the work of ministry. This meant that even in smaller congregations pastors trained individuals to conduct congregational care. These people did and continue to do many of the care tasks often identified as something pastors are expected to perform.

This new structure also meant a new way of looking at church boards. Their responsibility was to govern, not manage or lead. They were to focus on the ends of ministry, goals set by the pastor and the pastor's staff members, not the means of ministry. The day-to-day conduct of ministry became the responsibility of staff members. Board members were taught that their job in relation to the pastor and the pastor's staff members were to be their protectors and cheerleaders. The board also held the pastor accountable each year for the missional goals that had been set by the pastor with the board's approval. However, the board was not to become involved in the management of the ministry. In fact we encouraged congregations to dissolve all committees and task forces. We encouraged a tradeoff between the effective accomplishment of a mission versus a bureaucracy that gave everyone a say regardless of whether ministry was accomplished effectively or not. In larger congregations we urged the pastor to hire an administrator who would oversee a team of people (both paid and volunteer) to handle many administrative responsibilities. However, this administrator reported to the pastor, not the board.

This new structure required that congregations of fifty, seventy, or 100 should be staff led. Most staff members were not paid, and if they were not retired they had full-time employment at other jobs during the week. These people were required to set behavioral, specific, and measurable goals for their respective areas of ministry. However, they were also given the complete authority, including the spending of their departmental budget allotments without special permission, to carry out their responsibilities. We trained them to recruit a team of individuals, they would develop as disciples and leaders to work with them. However, we made it quite clear that each staff member would be held accountable for the goals that had been established, not the team. It was, and continues to be, amazing how lay volunteers act when they are treated respectfully as staff members who are given the freedom to direct their ministries in relation to goals. They recruit whomever they want to be on their team and are responsible to see that these individuals get the training they need to be effective in ministry. These staff members no longer see themselves as volunteers, but as people ministering alongside the pastor to accomplish the mission and vision of the congregation. By the way, it is possible to fire such staff members if they fail to meet their goals.

These five issues, challenging smaller congregations to act the size they want to become, becoming outward focused in mission, developing a vision to change a community, adopting values aligned with an outwardly mission and vision, and developing a structure that enhances an outward mission and vision were fundamental to helping congregations move from spiritual and organizational dysfunction to spiritual and organizational health. The agenda I and other consultants had in conducting consultations was to use the consultation process to persuade congregations to embrace these five key issues. The result was that we observed a large number of congregations respond positively to these five fundamental issues related to change. We experienced an approximate seventy-five percent rate of change among the congregations with whom we consulted.

Protecting the Risk Takers

In the previous chapter I mentioned that we replaced conflict mediation with congregational consultations. The reason I gave is that mediation deals with conflict while consultations dealt with control. When congregations are in decline or on a plateau those controlling it need to be replaced with those who will lead it to grow. Such action often creates friction. When this friction occurs it is important for those with influence to use it to protect the new leaders from the former leaders who would often rather be in positions of influence than see health and growth occur. I felt that we in the region needed to take on this role of protecting the new leaders. We then found that often many in the congregation who were neutral to the changes embraced the new behaviors once they had the time to see how effective they were in producing health, vitality, and growth.

In our congregational consultations our goal was to establish the pastor as the leader of the congregation. At the same time the pastor had to be willing to be held accountable for specific missional goals. If the goals were met the pastor was given even more freedom to lead. If the goals were not met, then the pastor needed to realize that perhaps a different calling and vocation was in the pastor's future. Several pastors have shared with me that as a result of the changes they have never had as much freedom to lead at any other time in their ministries while at the same time being held to a much higher standard of accountability.

The pastor then appointed staff members to oversee those ministries that people expected congregations to perform with some degree of excellence. Most people enter congregations as consumers, seeking how a particular congregation will meet their needs. We felt that this mindset was partially appropriate and partially inappropriate. Individuals should expect congregations to have great worship, good teaching for different age levels, groups where people can make friends, and more. However, if this is all the people are given, the leadership of the congregation is pandering to their consumer mentality. Therefore, like missionaries, staff member are employed to develop teams of people to meet these needs in order to keep people coming. The reason the leadership wants to keep people coming is so they will be challenged to participate in the mission and vision of changing a community by making more disciples for Jesus Christ.

All of these changes eventually produced resistance, either as it was being implemented or after people realized that groups and individuals were functioning differently. It was at this point that we protected those leaders who were taking risks by putting their reputations on the line to be held accountable for specific accomplishments. Often it meant meeting with board members to help them understand how they were to protect their pastor and allowing the pastor to lead. At other times it meant meeting with congregations and helping them understand that the new ways of functioning by the pastor, the new staff members, and the board were crucial to implementing the outwardly focused mission and vision they said they desired. We often reminded leaders of commitments they had made either during the consultation or at some point after it. Sometimes protecting congregational leaders meant meeting with pastors to remind them that, since they now had both the authority and responsibility for ministry, if goals were not met they were accountable and could not shift the blame to others.

We were helping pastors, leaders, and congregations function in entirely new ways, employ new paradigms of ministry, and seek new goals. Therefore, we were constantly helping them adjust both in relation to their own specific responsibilities and the responsibilities and expectations of others. We were also showing them that things that were no longer happening were not that important and had ceased to provide productive results in the past. Sometimes our protection meant shielding them from old habits and behaviors that would have scuttled the new mission and vision.

Broadening the Protection

We also needed to protect pastors, lay leaders, and even congregations from other pastors, congregations, and denominational leaders. Often those who were resistant to our changes or had not yet experienced a congregational consultation and were observing from afar reacted negatively to things they perceived as either threatening or not the normal Baptist way of conducting ministry. In many cases the perceptions were incomplete and those criticizing had assumed the worst in both behavior and motive. These complaints often surfaced at regional events or meetings. Our job was to provide explanations to the critics, often correcting misinformation, while offering protection to those risking change. We often protected the risk takers by informing the critics that these congregations and leaders were simply doing what we had encouraged. We also pointed out that the changes were the norm for congregations across the country that desired to move from dysfunction to health. By doing this, we directed any anger or frustration at us instead of at the congregation making the changes.

The environment in our denomination is slowly changing. However, during the four years of intervention we had to protect our congregations from people in positions of leadership elsewhere in our denomination. Often when a congregation was going through major systemic changes, those resisting it came to the region seeking help for their cause. When they found that we would not help them they went to people in national positions and brought complaints. Often that which was said was based upon misinformation of incorrect perceptions or an outright distortion of the facts. The national denominational people at that time handled these complaints in such a way that triangulation occurred. By this I mean we, as leaders in a region, were never informed of specific complaints and who was making them so we could deal with them. Instead we were just told that important people in our region were complaining and we should probably change what we were doing so that this would stop.

Our way of protecting those congregations and leaders from the pressure at national levels was to handle them the way Nehemiah did. Often when Nehemiah was criticized by his enemies he said that he could not stop to argue since the work was too important. For the most part we ignored their criticisms and told our pastors and congregations not to worry about it. I took on as part of my task as Executive Minister the handling of the critiques and the critics and not telling anyone else in the region so they could keep on leading congregations to health and growth. I would talk to people at the national office when they wanted to meet and try and explain what we were doing. However, I did not go out of my way to deal with rumors or gossip. We just let it fly and said one day the truth will come out. After all, due to triangulation we had no idea who the actual people were who were complaining about what issues. The result of all this was that eventually our national board voted to send a team of people to look into all the negative things they were hearing about our region.

Two good things came out of this team visit. One, the team determined that there was no substance to the negative and inflammatory comments that had been made and often repeated regularly. Second, their report is now leading to a process of dealing with regional issues at the national level directly, rather than through triangulation. This different way of functioning is already being practiced by our new General Secretary who is creating a new and better atmosphere for the conduct of ministry in our denomination.

The bottom line is that systemic congregational change will create criticism both from within and outside the congregations making the changes. The role of judicatory leaders, particularly if they are leading that change, is to protect those taking the risks. One advantage that congregations in denominations have over those with no connection to a denomination, or even those with a loose affiliation in a fellowship, is that many of the long-time members in the congregations have a strong allegiance to the denomination. This allegiance needs to be leveraged to help produce change by allowing such members to see that the judicatory leaders are both leading the change and supporting the changes that congregations are making.

Moving from Competition to Cooperation

The third strategy we used to help our congregations realize that they were and are God's primary unit of mission was to create and atmosphere of interdependence. Too often pastors and in some cases congregations see themselves as competing with others in their judicatory. This mindset often becomes exaggerated when the congregations are declining and there is a premium on the few people we have attending and supporting financially the needs of the congregation. We knew that we needed to change the mindset from one of competition to cooperation and interdependence. After all, the ultimate goal is a body of congregations who individually and corporately are seeking to fulfill the Great Commission.

However, tactics were developed intentionally to foster an interdependent attitude between congregations and pastors. The first one related to the covenant we asked congregations to sign when they were selected as one of the seven to ten congregations their area consultant would work with intensely for a year. The covenant required the leaders of that particular congregation to assist area consultants in their work with other congregations that would be selected the following year. Therefore, we had already begun to build in cooperation. We told the current congregational leaders that in the following year they would be asked to meet with other boards and individuals in other congregations to share what they had learned and how they had handled similar issues related to the change process.

A second deliberate tactic related to the conduct of pastoral cluster meetings. Part of the training process was to have pastors from the congregations that were being worked with intentionally share both what was happening and how they were attacking different problems related to change. The area consultant then asked for input and guidance from other pastors about how they would deal with certain issues. A number of the pastors responding were either going through the change process at the same time or would be in the next year or so. The result was that often cluster meetings became peer group learning events where the best practices, for leading change, was the focus. Every pastor realized that she or he was in the same boat or soon would be. In fact in some clusters pastors began to come with an eager anticipation of sharing victories or finding help for immediate problems. The good news was that the problems were related to changing congregations. The discussions were being conducted at an entirely new level.

A third tactic was to tell stories to congregations wrestling with change about how other congregations dealing with similar issues had fared. Area consultants often worked as brokers connecting people in one congregation with individuals in another congregation so they could share about the successful resolution of common problems. This practice has become a common behavior among leaders. For example, a small, highly dysfunctional congregation formerly led by a pastor who had actively worked against the mission of the region came to us for help. The pastor had left and the leaders kept hearing how congregations were successfully negotiating change. After leading them through a congregational consultation I asked our consultant to set up three meetings with other congregations near them that had at one time been small, highly dysfunctional, filled with conflict, and led by highly ineffective pastors. However, recently those congregations had turned around, were becoming healthy, growing to the point of having multiple worship services, and experiencing numerous baptisms each year. In those meetings leaders shared with leaders how they had gone through the change process well. The result was yet another congregation navigating change with great success. In this process we were able to foster a strong spirit of cooperation and interdependence among four congregations.

A fourth tactic related to my work with Leith Anderson in creating Teaching Church Network. I brought a number of our more effective pastors together and asked them if they would be willing to mentor other pastors and congregations through the change process. Two results came out of this meeting. First, we established a teaching congregational mentality where congregations worked together like a congregational consultant to help lead other congregations through the change process. In one case a team of eleven, three pastors and eight lay leaders, from three growing congregations who had broken the 200 barrier did a congregational consultation with a congregation of seventy. The result of that year's work enabled this congregation, which had been on a plateau for years to begin to grow and have over 100 in average worship attendance. It also fostered tremendous cooperation between the four congregations.

The second result has changed the very way we lead pastors in our region. Several years ago a number of our larger congregational pastors agreed to become mentors to other pastors in the region. We established special clusters where selected pastors would leave the pastoral cluster in which they normally met in order to meet with a mentoring pastor. Each mentoring pastor developed his own curriculum and usually worked with the same group of pastors for a one- to two-year period. The results and feedback were extremely positive. This act created a great sense of cooperation and interdependence between the pastors with the mentoring pastor and with each other.

The mentoring pastor idea worked so effectively that I asked approximately twenty pastors to be mentoring pastors. I selected pastors who were leading their congregations to change and grow. I wanted pastors also who were leading congregations that were either over or had broken the 200 barrier. I also wanted pastors who had demonstrated a commitment to the region's mission and vision. These pastors, rather than region staff members, are now leading all of our monthly pastoral clusters. I am now partnering with a former Executive Minister from another Baptist group, who had led his district to growth and health to oversee this endeavor. He is responsible for overseeing the mentors, developing a region-wide curriculum, and being a coach to the coaches. We now conduct three meetings a year just for our mentors and their spouses. The meetings are designed to help them develop as mentors and to provide other resources they can use as leaders of their own congregations. We pay our mentoring pastors and I treat them as an extension of our region's staff.

One of the most rewarding comments I hear from those outside our circles who come to investigate what we are doing, is that our pastors and congregations do not compete with each other; rather they work together.

The Church of Jesus Christ is usually identified with local congregations. It is through these local congregations that God's mission of making more disciples for Jesus Christ is usually accomplished. The congregation truly is God's primary unit of mission.

Judicatories must behave and act in such a way that this belief becomes reality. We do not transform congregations; only congregations transform themselves. We do not plant congregations. Congregations are to reproduce and plant new ones. However, in our leadership role we can be the catalytic agent that leads, encourages, resources, and helps congregations become what God intended. Our judicatories do not exist to serve our denomination. Rather we are denominations who exist to serve our congregations.

Chapter Five
Discovering Gold by Finding New Leaders

A PIECE OF OUR STORY

The vitality of the congregation is related to the quality of leadership being provided by the pastor of the congregation. For us to create an environment of health and growth we knew we needed to raise the quality of leadership among the majority of our current pastors. However, we also believed that such an environment required us to recruit to the region pastors who were proven leaders. We needed to find pastors who already had track records of leading congregations into health, vital ministry, and growth.

We invited a rather young pastor to come to our region and consider leading a very unhealthy congregation. This pastor had a track record of growing ministries where ever he had been. He had led effective youth ministries and was leading a growing congregation in an American Baptist region that was not growing or seeing a lot of health and growth in its congregations.

The congregation where we asked this pastor to interview had gone through three congregational splits in the last decade. The current congregation averaged about seventy in attendance and was close to sixty in average age. This pastor was willing to leave the growing congregation where he was. Six years later the congregation is averaging over 400 in attendance, has multiple worship services, and is getting ready to help plant a new congregation.

This story has now been repeated over forty times in our region. Over eighty percent of the congregations that these "growth" pastors have come to lead are growing. The rest are in the process of being turned around and are experiencing the initial healthy changes that lead to growth.

The work these new pastors are doing in leading congregations, added to the efforts of pastors who have been in the region, confirm, again that

leadership is the human key issue. Good leaders produce effective ministry and lead healthy congregations. Poor leaders are not only ineffective, they assist congregations in creating even greater dysfunction.

If a new way of thinking about leadership and finding leaders for judicatories is required in order to see them again become effective in ministry, the same is true for congregations. I believe that good or poor leadership determines effectiveness or ineffectiveness in ministry. The traditional model of leadership that we have held up for pastoral leaders, a perverted model of shepherding, is not only unbiblical but quite ineffective. It produces small inwardly focused congregations that basically give into a consumer mindset of taking care of the blessed before reaching out to those who are spiritually sick and desperate. It also produces co-dependent pastors who may say that they are frustrated with laity, who sit and expect to be served while at the same time meeting ego-fulfilling needs of the pastor as the overall giver of care and service.

There are exceptions where congregations have experienced a turn-around without a pastor. We have experienced such exceptions in the region. However, a key in moving from dysfunction to health is finding the right leader. This was even true in changed congregations who had no pastor to lead the change. I do believe this is a foundational biblical principle. The New Testament speaks of the gift of leadership, the role of leaders, and expects congregations to be led. How such leaders are compensated, qualified, and even function in relation to other leaders may be up for debate. However, leadership is required.

In this chapter I develop the strategies and tactics we used to develop, find, and maintain high quality pastoral leaders. Our first strategy was to develop an intentional leadership program for pastors. We implemented a number of tactics to develop lay leaders. However, our focus was on the role of the pastor as leader. A second strategy was and is related to how we attract new leaders to the region. Every judicatory leader recognizes that the vitality of the judicatory is directly related to the caliber of pastors leading the congregations. A third strategy was related to the structures we have and are setting in place to continually develop the leaders we have, attract new leaders, and maintain leadership as a high and non-negotiable value.

Making Leadership a Value

Prior to the intervention in our region, those who led well were not seen as the heroes of the region. Instead the focus was often on the smaller congregational pastors who maintained a family atmosphere across the region. If there were congregational problems the usual assumption was that it was the pastor's fault. After doing conflict mediation the pastor was usually encouraged to leave since it was easier to fire the pastor than the congregation. However, the pastor was not confronted about her or his ability to lead, and if any help was offered it assumed a shepherd model that encouraged a pastor to simply do a better job of caring for the sheep

We insisted that leadership has one basic criterion, and that is whether anyone is really following or not. Because of our Baptist heritage there was a strong fear of giving the leader too much authority to lead. Many laypeople felt that if pastors were given too much authority they would misuse it and become dictatorial in their behavior. Most of our congregational and regional structures were designed to prevent abuse of authority. Related to this fear was the value of giving everyone an equal right to speak, whether they were informed or not, or had earned that right or not. Therefore, any kind of leadership that in any way inhibited this right to have a say was improper.

So for two years we promoted the idea that effective or ineffective ministry is directly related to good or poor leadership. Nearly all the training and trainers that we brought in for region-wide training events talked about leadership. Regional staff members were encouraged to take the training they were receiving and share it each month in their cluster meetings with pastors. Most of the materials we purchased for our Resource Center were on the topic of leadership. When we met with congregations, boards, or other congregational leaders we talked about mission, vision, and leadership. In fact we made it clear that a new mission and vision would not be achieved without leadership. The Executive Minister began to write a monthly newsletter aimed primarily at pastors entitled "Leadership Lines."

The goal of regional leaders was to marry the concept of effective leadership to the development of healthy, growing congregations, which was the region's new mission. Other American Baptist regions have and are trying things to help congregations and their regions turn around. This emphasis is also pursued in other judicatories in other denominations. Perhaps our experience can help these regions move beyond the information and into transformation. In part our strategies succeeded because we did not only talk intellectually about congregational health and growth. We did bring in the right people to lead training events in congregational systems and ministries, but we first focused on the leadership issue and made that a concrete priority, with measurement and accountability.

Renewal is related to two different disciplines of knowledge. There is a large body of material related to leadership and how it should be understood and implemented well. Then there is another wide body of knowledge related to congregational health and growth. Too often we only focus on the congregational knowldge base without focusing on the leadership practices. Moving from dysfunction to health demands **courage**, **passion**, and the **willingness** to risk, coupled with an understanding of the basic principles required for change and how to lead change. It also requires the wisdom to implement these principles with both skill and courage. Too often I believe we have asked people who are not leaders, or have not been trained to be leaders, to lead such dangerous change.

Developing Shepherds into Leaders

While intensive training convinced pastors that they were not called to be chaplains of congregations but leaders, other training events were designed for lay leaders. Lay leaders were also invited to training events for pastors. As a result lay leaders realized that the pastor's job is not to manage congregational ministries but lead them. Having the laity hear the same message as pastors was helpful in changing mind-sets. While good results were apparent, it was not enough; we had to come at leadership development in a variety of ways.

I have already mentioned that pastoral clusters were used to train pastors in their responsibilities as leaders. However, in clusters the training was developed somewhat differently. Through the use of case studies and actual congregational situations there were numerous opportunities for hands-on teaching. In monthly meetings the clusters also provided a way to hold pastors accountable for creating new behaviors.

Another tactic required regional staff members to model leadership in the clusters so that pastors could see what was expected of them. When I came to the region I led four clusters. All of them were filled with pastors who wanted to spend most of the time sharing their problems rather than discussing how they or their congregations might improve. Instead, I chose to act differently and began bringing resources to help them grow and develop. I knew that if they began to view me as an excellent trainer, providing materials that would enable them to be better at what they did, they would allow me to lead them. By the way, this is how I served them. I did not pander to their negativity and lack of hope by simply listening and commiserating with them. Instead I injected hope into our meetings. I did this by working hard at both preparing materials and then presenting those materials in ways that enabled pastors to go home and implement new behaviors that worked and produced results. Because of this service they allowed me to be their leader.

I also served pastors by being a regional representative who would come into their congregation when needed and speak the truth to people who still behaved in dysfunctional ways. Often members of the congregation wanted change but had no idea how to function differently so change could occur. At other times boards needed assistance in seeing the big picture and how specific actions or even inaction would inhibit them from implementing behaviors that would produce the big picture. Often I have gone to board meetings and asked the pastor ahead of time what I needed to say that, if the pastor said it, might lead the board to consider dismissing the pastor. In functioning this way I became the pastor's defender and

therefore the pastor's leader. I also served the congregation by helping them adopt behaviors that avoided more dysfunction while
leading to health. It also modeled how the pastor might need to
function in future situations in the congregation. Again, by serving
the pastor and the mission of the congregation at the expense of my
reputation, the pastor allowed me to lead.

Being the leader of pastors meant then that I could then begin to
expect them to lead. This meant taking risks, acting courageously,
and learning what was important both about leadership and about
what to lead and what to ignore.

I always assume the best in every cluster meeting of every pastor
regardless of how poorly the pastor thought about his or her ability
to lead. I constantly envisioned a better future and what these pastors would be doing some day to lead healthy, growing, and effective
ministries. I believed they all could develop as leaders. Some might
develop better than others and accomplish more as leaders; however I really did believe they each could improve. I found that by treating pastors this way and expecting the best, they did improve and
some have even surpassed my greatest expectations for them.

In addition to clusters I used congregational consultations as a
major tactic to get pastors to think and act as leaders. One reason
I wanted to meet with them for an extended time prior to the consultation was to discuss a number of leadership issues. First I wanted to revisit with them past events where, if they had led differently or led at all, they might not be currently facing the pain they
were. Many pastors back off from the tough acts of leadership
because they do want to experience the pain. However, they do not
avoid the pain since failure to lead in the past contributes to dysfunction in the present.

Second, I wanted to ascertain whether the pastor was planning to
stay once the consultation was over. If, in my opinion, the current
pastor was a major impediment to future health, then I needed to
know whether that pastor was planning for a long-term commitment or not. If the pastor was staying then I needed to let the pastor know my concern. However, if the pastor was leaving then I

wanted to make sure I did what I could to help the pastor leave well. However, the more usual case was the pastor was staying and required help to lead the congregation through the turnaround. I wanted to then share with the pastor what I believed the key leadership issues to be, what the pastor would need to do to lead well, and the potential fallout that might occur even if the pastor led well. I also wanted a commitment from the pastor and the pastor's spouse to be willing to stay and see the change through to completion. I told pastors not to start the change process if they were going to leave in the middle when things might be most difficult.

As I was interviewing pastor and spouse to ascertain their commitment to remain with the congregation after the consultation I would be very explicit with them. I would point out the issues in the past where the pastor failed to lead. Now sometimes that was the pastor's fault and on other occasions it was because certain leaders would not let the pastor lead. Then I would talk about what the pastor would need to do in the next few months after the consultation to demonstrate that the pastor would be the leader. At that point I told the pastor that no one but God now knows whether the pastor can lead effectively or not. The test will be in the next several months to see if the pastor has the courage, the wisdom, and the skills to take advantage of the situations produced through the consultation. I would say that if the pastor fails to lead, then the pastor needs to consider other career or ministry options. However, I would tell the pastor that we would be there to walk with her or him, and that our goal was to have them succeed.

We have now learned to set goals for the pastor to achieve in the next six months to a year with the understanding that if most of the goals are not achieved the pastor needs to consider leaving that congregation. I have found that by being clear up front, it is easier to discuss the future with the pastor if things do not go well.

Third, I wanted the pastor to know that he or she would not be left alone to lead change once the consultation was over. Either I or another consultant would be there to walk with them as they led change. If I conducted the consultation and therefore knew a lot about the congregation and had interacted significantly with key leaders they could always call me even if another consultant was working with them throughout the year. I would be asking them to take some big risks as the leader. Therefore it was crucial that I provide support, encouragement, and assistance.

During the consultation itself I wanted to model leadership for the pastor. Usually the pastor had been with those in leadership positions long enough to know them and what their particular concerns, fears, and issues were. I also knew that I had advantages as an outsider since I was usually viewed as an expert. However, I did not have the experience that came with interacting with this particular group of leaders over time. Therefore, I wanted the pastor to see how I listened and treated people with respect. Yet while listening and showing respect I wanted the pastor to observe that I did not back away from the truth. I needed to confront issues in a loving way in order to enable the congregation to begin to move in the right direction. I wanted the pastor to watch someone whose devotion to the mission of the congregation could not be swayed. Yet at the same time I needed to demonstrate a deep desire to see people fulfilled as disciples because they embraced Christ's mission. The pastor often needed to see a model of someone who let the mission dictate behavior not people. Also, I wanted the pastor to see someone who would not avoid the difficult leadership choices. If confrontation was needed, whether in a group or individual setting, I needed to demonstrate that I would take on that responsibility and, hopefully, handle it well.

The ongoing months of working with the pastor and congregational leaders was as much a time of pastoral leadership development as it was for congregational change. Usually in meeting regularly with the pastor I spent as much time working on how the pastor would lead in different circumstances as what the pastor and leaders needed to do. For example we would often have people take on new behaviors and responsibilities and then act as though no change had occurred. In many cases it was simply a habitual response from the past while in others it was done in anger or malice. Every such case needed a response that was appropriate to the situation. However in each case the pastor had to respond as a leader. Often I helped the pastor first realize the implications of what had just taken place and the ramifications of ignoring it. Second, I let the pastor know what action was required, who should be involved, and how the encounter needed to be handled. In such cases I usually had the pastor contact me immediately after the event in order to make sure that no further damage control was needed.

Changing the pastoral mindset from chaplain to leader happened through a variety of tactics. One was the constant training we exposed pastors to through leaders we brought into the region. Second, we used the clusters as a peer group learning process for pastors to wrestle with individual situations in their own congregations. Third, the consultation process, which involved working with pastors for a year, created the opportunity to mentor pastors in leadership. This mentoring took place in a real-life situation where the learning was implemented immediately.

Recruiting New Leaders

I am convinced that most pastors seeking to lead new congregations do not know how to go about that task well. Usually the pastor wanted out of the current situation because things were not going well and as a result negotiated with any new search committees from a perspective of weakness. Congregations for the most part did not know how to search well for new pastors. Too often they assumed that since this person had a seminary degree, had led another congregation, and handled his or her interviews well, this person was qualified to lead their congregation. Usually a pastor left a smaller congregation to become pastor at at slightly larger congregations, which meant that the pastor was hired on the basis of potential rather than experience.

As I shared these thoughts with other staff members we developed a strategy that has revolutionized our region. We all agreed that the best time to persuade a congregation about its need to turn from dysfunctional behavior to a healthier way of acting was when the current pastor left. We also knew as Baptists that we could not command congregations to act in certain ways and that we had to attract them to do what we believed was best. We also knew that we needed to attract to our region good young leaders who understood congregational health and growth. Finally, we also knew that recent seminary graduates would not be the answer, because neither we nor they knew if they could lead well.

The strategy we developed offered congregations two options when they were faced with the situation of finding a new pastor. The tradition in our region was one where an area consultant would work with a congregation from the beginning to the end of the search process. We used this tradition but changed it to fit our strategy and tactics. We offered congregations a modified version of our traditional way of functioning. However, a congregation could also select an entirely new strategy designed to help them find a pastor who was a leader and understood congregational health and growth. We deliberately make the latter option more attractive than the older traditional method, so that congregations would select it. The majority of the congregations have chosen the newer strategy.

In the traditional process congregations through their region contact the personnel system developed by American Baptists for pastoral transitions. We helped them get anywhere from fifty to 150 profiles of potential pastoral candidates. It was at this juncture we deviated from the former way of functioning. First, we told the congregation that it would be their responsibility to form a search committee, cull through the pastoral profiles, decide how they would select potential candidates, and what process they would need to develop to interview and select an eventual pastor. Normally, regional staff members had worked with them through this entire process. That would no longer be true because we felt this process to be highly flawed and ineffective.

Second, we informed them that the candidate pool from which they would be fishing for a prospect was quite shallow. Not shallow in terms of the numbers of candidates, unless the congregation was quite small, in a rural location, and could not provide adequate compensation. The pool was quite shallow in terms of the quality of the candidates that congregations could expect to interview. Our denomination is declining in the number of congregations, the congregations are declining in size, and our congregations as a norm are aging and not attracting new growth. Therefore, if a particular congregation thinks that our profile system is going to provide a good leader who understands growth and health, that congregation is generally mistaken. The best leaders do not use the profile system, since they do not need it, and most pastors in the profile system are looking for positions because effective ministry is not happening where they are currently located. In other words congregations are looking for pastoral leaders who, with some exceptions, are devoid of either leadership abilities, training, or understanding.

If a congregation wanted to go the traditional route, regional staff members would provide the profiles, but the rest was up to the congregation. A few congregations continue to take this option. Seldom has a congregation been able to find a good leader. Some have done well, but most have not.

The second option we offered congregations is titled "Growth Track." This option involved an intentional covenant relationship between the region and the congregation. However, before we even offered this option we asked pastors to tell their area consultant first that they would be leaving or retiring. If this occurred, a regional staff member was with them when they informed the board. The purpose for this was to provide the regional staff member an opportunity to explain to board members the grief process that needed to be followed when well-loved pastors leave. If the opposite was the case, the staff member helped the board members develop a process to let the pastor leave well, even if the pastor was not well liked by most of the congregation. Second, the regional staff member explained the options we offered congregations, which are the "Traditional" model and the "Growth Track" model. If the board members opted for the "Growth Track" model the area consultant met with them again and gave them a notebook that spelled out all the expectations, and the covenant of agreement between the region and the congregation, which was signed.

In the "Growth Track" model the area consultant asked the board with the addition of a few other people to be the search committee. We then led the congregation through a congregational consultation. One other element we added to the consultation was the creation of a pastoral profile, once the initial consultation weekend was over. We also led the congregation through an envisioning day to help them develop a new vision for the future. If we felt it was necessary we recommended a transitional interim whose primary responsibility was to come in and lead the congregation through the implementation of the consultation prescriptions.

| Pastoral Search Processes ||
Traditional Track	Growth Track
Consultant meets to explain processes	Consultant meets to explain processes
No exit strategy	Develop an exit strategy
No grief process	Develop a grief process for congregation
No assessment	Conduct an assessment and perform a consultation
No envisioning	Conduct an envisioning day
Congregation puts together search committee	Board with others becomes search committee and is instructed in procedure
Committee puts together pastoral profile; consultant will help if asked.	Consultant helps develop pastoral profile based on the consultation with search committee
Consultant contacts ABC Profile System and provides congregation with profiles of candidates	Region staff begin to look for potential pastors for interviews with search committee
Search committee on its own in finding pastor	Growth pastors interview with committee until one is selected and then interviews begin
Search committee calls pastor	Search committee calls pastors and region staff help prepare the way for congregational interaction and involvement
Congregation votes	Congregation votes
Pastor installed	Pastor installed
No six-month follow-up	Region offers staff follow-up with congregation after six months

At this point in the process regional staff members began to network with leaders across the country to locate potential growth pastors to come and interview with the search committee about leading this congregation. Ideally we wanted to bring in three potential growth pastors to interview with three different congregational search committees during the same week. If in one of the interviews there was enough interest between the pastor and the search committee to have a second interview, all other contacts with congregations and potential pastors were stopped. If after the second interview interest was still there, then the candidating process began. However, if there were no connections with any of the congregations or with any of the potential pastors, then we on staff began the networking process again to locate more potential pastors. This process continued until the congregation settled on a new pastor and the new pastor was installed as the leader of that particular congregation.

Elements of the "Growth Track" Process

Why a Covenant: Executive Ministers in Baptist circles are not bishops. We do not select or install pastors for local congregations.[1] Since each congregation is autonomous and selects its own pastor we can only recommend and bring whatever influence we have to bear on what the leaders of a congregation will ultimately decide. The purpose of the covenant, however, was to lay out expectations of what we would and could do as a region and what was expected of the congregation. This option took much more commitment of time, energy, and financial resources of the region then the traditional method. (Money from the two million dollars set aside for training and recruitment was spent on travel expenses, bringing in potential candidates for congregations that could not afford to pay.) However, since the local congregation was our focus, the investment was worth it and would pay great spiritual dividends for both the congregation and the region. Part of the covenant discussed the future relationship with the region in terms of how the new pastor would be a part of what we were doing and what the congregation would do in sending missions dollars. This whole process was a way of creating a better relationship between the region and the congregation.

The Board as the Search Committee: Asking the board of the congregation to be the search committee solved a number of potential problems. In congregations where pastors are not appointed it is common to create an ad hoc search committee. It is also common for this committee to be fairly large, since often the thinking is that all the major groups in the congregation need to be represented; youth, seniors, singles, young marrieds, and different ministries. Traditionally the committee meets, establishes the search process, begins to examine profiles, selects candidates, sets up interviews, and finally establishes how the candidating process will function.

Once the candidate becomes the pastor the ad hoc committee normally disbands. The candidate, who is now the pastor, has interacted with this committee, negotiated with this committee, and often received implied promises and commitments from this committee. However, it is not the group the new pastor will work with once the pastor is installed. Therefore all agreements, negotiations, and promises are null and void. It is much like buying a new muffler for your car and receiving a lifetime guarantee, only to realize that when there is a problem the muffler store has gone out of business and been replaced by a shop that sells doughnuts.

If the board is the committee then the pastor and the board live with any commitments, explicit or implied, once the candidate becomes the pastor. Those negotiating with the new pastor know they are the ones who will be working with the new pastor.

A second problem often is the large size of the committee. In trying to get all vested interests in the congregation represented, the committee is usually quite large. We knew that whenever you have more than ten people in a meeting, only two or three really make the key decisions and those decisions are normally not made in the meeting. They are made in the parking lot, over the telephone, or in private conversations after worship on a Sunday morning. Also, if this group does function well you then get a pastor who meets the lowest common denominator, since everyone needs to sign off on the candidate. Usually after a congregational consultation we encouraged congregations to have smaller boards of no more than three to seven people. Therefore, if a board of seven added three representatives from the congregation to be part of the search process the group still only had ten people on it.

We also encouraged congregations to have individuals sit on the board to represent the mission and vision rather than special interest groups. We want this commitment modeled in the search process as well. Too often in congregations board and pastors are seen in an adversarial relationship. We wanted to change that by creating a leadership community. (See Chapter 6.) However, having a search committee that was a different group than the board fostered the older concept of board versus pastor.

Developing a Pastoral Profile: The purpose of a congregational consultation is to provide leaders with the specific strengths and weaknesses of the congregation. We also provided leaders with specific prescriptions of what the congregation needed to do in order to become healthy and accomplish an outward focused mission. In the case of a congregation without a pastor we also developed a pastoral profile. The profile also took into account those unique features of that congregation that related to its history, its community, the culture of the congregation, and the specific way God was leading people to implement the mission and vision.

Employing Intentional Interims: In many instances during the consultation we came to the conclusion that the congregation needed an intentional interim to come in immediately and begin implementing the prescriptions the consultant had recommended. In some rare cases a long-tenured pastor had retired and the congregation needed some time to grieve and heal. In many cases the congregation was either so conflicted or demoralized that they needed someone with gray hair and wisdom to lead them. Another reason was to take advantage of the momentum that had been created through the consultation and envisioning process.

We trained some interims to fill this role. These retired pastors knew that their responsibility was not to come in and hold the fort and comfort the congregation. Instead their job was to come in and begin leading the congregation in the change process. They were to trade on their wisdom and gray hair and use it to leverage change particularly with those long-term members who were unsure of all that was happening. These interim leaders could take all the criticism that comes with change so that when the growth pastor arrived many of the tough issues had already been tackled. We were asking them to take all the arrows in the back that they could stand and then leave. To their credit a number of these retired pastors have done just that. They have worked hard at becoming leaders and learning about congregational health and growth as well as what it takes to lead a congregation through change. These pastors are "velvet covered bricks." They are some of the unsung heroes of our turnaround.

Recruiting "Growth Track" Pastors: The most difficult part of the "Growth Track" process was recruiting the pastors. That is still true today. The major difficulty is that the pastors we seek are not looking to leave their congregation at the time. No one has a list of these persons. Everything was done through networking. Another major difficulty we faced was our basic criterion for such a pastor. The person we wanted needed to be leading a growing congregation that was larger than the one we were calling this individual to lead in our region. This does not fit the norm of how pastors or congregations normally look at pastoral advancement. Our model is based on experience, not potential. It was a wiser guess to assume that a pastor could come to a congregation of 150 and lead it to 400 if the pastor already had experience with 400. We have not always been able to stick to the criteria we established. We have made exceptions for associate staff who have been involved in large ministries or people who have developed and led larger ministries that may not have been congregations. But in almost all cases we have followed the experience model over the potential model.

We trained our congregations to seek people who would normally not be seeking them. Therefore the search committee was not in the driver's seat in the negotiation process; rather the candidate was. The candidate was already leading an effective, successful ministry and did not need to even consider this position. Thus the search committee had to develop a pastoral search brochure that would attract such pastors. It needed to be developed as a marketing tool that was designed to interest highly attractive candidates. It had to describe how they were changing, open to change, and how they wanted to be a mission and vision led congregation. In essence the brochure had to make the congregation attractive to someone who would not be easily impressed.

The search committee also had to learn that the interview process was not an interrogation of the candidate but rather the candidate interrogating them. With the board as the search committee, they were forced to answer difficult questions by the candidates. We even laid out potential interview questions for search committees in order to get them to think and function differently. We also did practice interviews using some of our more effective pastors to coach the committee in developing a good interview process. Also, after each actual interview we evaluated with and for the committee their strengths and weaknesses. We wanted each interview to be a learning experience for the committee.

We in the region had two problems. First, finding the candidates is one of my primary tasks as the Executive Minister, although I use all the contacts I have in the region. I find it is either feast or famine. Usually a new pastor will bring more new contacts from that pastor's network. There are even times when I have hired friends with more contacts than me to act as "head hunters." Second, explaining the vision for a turn around to the candidates was more difficult earlier on than it is now. We currently have a number of pastors who say they will never leave this region. They are supported and encouraged in ways they never thought possible or experienced in other regions. We have them talk to potential new pastors. However, in the first few years we did not have a group of raving fans. Therefore we painted the vision of where the region was going, what God was going to do, and how new pastors coming as leaders could get in on the ground floor and be an integral part of this new venture. Another selling point was how we were preparing congregations through the consultation, the envisioning, and through transitional interims to be ready for a pastor who would lead them to growth and health. Obviously God blessed and we now have a large and growing number of pastors who caught the vision and are helping us reach the great mission field of Northern California, North-west Nevada, and abroad.

Another issue was compensation. First, pastors were leaving larger congregations to come to smaller ones, and we believed they should get a raise for this, not take a loss. Second, many were leaving parts of the country where property values and living conditions were less expensive than our part of the nation. Therefore, we used some of the two million dollars we had freed up and created a revolving loan procedure for congregations. Congregations could borrow up to $24,000 for two years to add to the compensation package they were offering the pastor. At the end of two years they would need to start paying this money back, interest free. We assumed that if the congregation was growing making these payments would not be excessive. That assumption has proven to be true.

Often one of the consultation prescriptions was to have our regional financial person lead the congregation through ways to increase their giving. To date the lowest increase we have seen the following year was a seventeen percent increase. This training then helped the congregation put together a compensation package that guaranteed the new pastor both a raise and proper compensation.

One final issue concerned the backgrounds of our pastors. Obviously we do not have enough pastors in American Baptist circles seeking to come to our region who would also meet our criteria for growth pastors. Therefore we had to be willing to go outside ABC circles to attract pastors. However, all our pastors had to agree to have their ordination recognized by the appropriate American Baptist entities. This influx of new blood from other circles has been a delight and a great enhancement to the ministry of the region.

Candidating and Installation: We were also involved to some degree in the actual interviewing process between the new pastor and the search committee. We wanted to ascertain that the committee was not tempted to revert to old habits of making this an interrogation. On the other hand we provided the committee the tough questions that are not often asked in such interviews. We also had the committee thoroughly check all references to make sure they did the work of discovering what was important and crucial about the candidate's background. We did act as a negotiator, if that role was needed in helping both parties develop an equitable compensation package.

Once the candidate and the committee agreed that this match was a good one we then worked with the committee to prepare for the candidate and the candidate's family to visit, meet, preach, and interact with the congregation. We had the committee develop a plan that made this time a win/win both for the candidate and the congregation. We made it clear to both the candidate and the committee that unless some major unforeseen issue arose both sides had already agreed to this match. Any vote by the congregation at the end of the process should really be a confirmation of all that had occurred up to that point.

The last part of the covenant agreement took place six months after the candidate was in place as the new pastor. We met again with both the pastor and board to ascertain how things were going. We used this time to make sure that any potential problems related to the new pastor leading change could be addressed in both an appropriate and healthy manner. The influx of new pastor leaders added to the growing number of pastors in the region has changed the very culture of the region. Our pastors' meetings are the most exciting ones we conduct since these leaders are always discussing mission, vision, conversions, making new disciples, and all the opportunities associated with growth.

---

[1] The traditional method of clergy placement in Baptist circles shares some elements in common with other denominations, including United Methodists, as follow: 1) moving clergy based on their unproven potential as they climb from smaller congregations to slightly larger congregations; 2) shuffling clergy when conflict occurs to another location within the region; 3) dependence upon the regional or district staff to supply a clergy candidate.

Chapter Six
Organizing Congregations for Mission

A PIECE OF OUR STORY

Prior to the intervention, the region was structured as a somewhat smaller version of our national bureaucracy. The region's board consisted of over fifty individuals who were elected to represent different geographical areas, various ministry interests, or institutions identified with the region. The region also had a number of committees, commissions, task forces, and institutional boards that met regularly for the purpose of conducting business and functioning as liaisons with national ministry entities. Much of the ministry of the region was related to planning meetings, conducting meetings, and reporting on meetings that had taken place. Each geographical area had its own program board that mirrored to some degree the structure of the region. Most of our congregations were structured like the region, with some having as many as three boards, multiple committees, along with other groups that had been created to oversee various ministry tasks. As congregations declined many of their organizational positions were either not filled or several people held multiple positions at the same time.

Our congregations were smaller versions of our regional bureaucracy. For example, one congregation which had averaged less than seventy people in worship for a decade had three boards. There was a board of deacons, trustees, and one for Christian education. There was also a variety of committees, each reporting to one of the boards. This aging congregation found it difficult to recruit enough people to fill all the board and committee positions. Most of the congregation's human resources were spent on maintaining the structure. Little time or energy was left for ministry and as a result most ministries were conducted ineffectively.

The congregations, the constituents of the region, voted at our annual meeting to suspend many parts of our regional by-laws. The parts they suspended related to who, how and when our committees, commissions, and task forces would be and when they would or would not meet. In other words, it was agreed that we would ignore much of our bureaucratic procedures. Some of these groups continued to meet, but only when there was specific business that needed a decision and the Executive Minister felt that he did not want to make that decision on his own. The business formerly handled by these groups was delegated to the Executive Minister and his staff. One ad hoc committee was formed at this point. This committee was given the responsibility of writing new by-laws that would create a new structure that reflected the new mission and vision and the new ways of conducting ministry in the region.

The constituents met three years later to adopt the new by-laws. This positive vote by the congregations resulted in numerous changes that affect the way the region functions currently. The region's board now consists of twenty-four members. All members now sit on the board as representatives of the mission and vision rather than as representatives of a number of diverse agendas. This new board only creates policy and delegates to the Executive Minister and his staff the implementation of these policies. There are only two commissions that function in the new structure, and they only meet when there is a need. The ordination commission meets when there are candidates that need to be examined. The commission on the ministry only meets when pastors and congregations have major moral or ethical issues that require region attention. Our two camps have boards that help them oversee their month-to-month operations. However those boards have no authority, and the two camp directors report directly to the Executive Minister.

There are now over 100 congregations that are structured this way and function in a similar manner to the region. The board creates policy, the pastor is the leader, and the pastor's staff is responsible to see that disciples are recruited, trained, and equipped to do the work of the ministry. These congregations have no ongoing committees or other administrative groups included in their structures.

The creation of new structures will never produce renewal in an organization. Renewal is instigated with a new mission, a compelling vision, and the adoption of new values. However, the change process is never ultimately achieved or solidified without the adoption of a new structure. In fact I would go further and suggest that the adoption of a new structure that is consistent with new mission, vision, and values accelerates the change process. Also failure to adopt a new structure will eventually stifle the implementation of a new mission and vision.

Structure is like a skeleton. If you can see your skeleton you are in serious trouble, yet without a skeleton you cannot function. Also, a skeleton that does not grow and develop produces great deformity and eventually death. (This is one major reason why so many congregations in North American are dying). Certain skeletons also limit the accomplishment of certain missions. For example a five-foot skeleton means that one will never play in the National Basketball Association regardless of that person's talents, intelligence, desire, or passion.

There is another important role that structure plays in the renewal of either judicatories or congregations. Mission, vision, and values are ultimately abstract concepts. They are an articulation of thinking, attitudes, priorities, beliefs, and feelings. That is why they are so powerful. Structure, on the other hand, is both abstract and tangible. When someone is given responsibilities to make certain decisions, that individual can actually hear the decision being made or see it written When we change structure we actually change what people can or cannot do, how they perform, and even what office they possess or lose. It causes people to either gain or lose influence over the way the organization functions. People as a result of changes in structure either lose or gain power, maintain or lose the ability to influence others, and gain or lose the ability to allocate resources. Therefore a change in structure is a tangible way of determining whether or not people are either embracing or denying new missions, visions, and values. A new structure is both a lightning rod and a thermometer of how well people are accepting or rejecting change. In other words, changes in structures create stress in people and that stress reveals where they stand in relation to the new changes. This phenomenon is why changes in structure that are aligned with new missions, visions, and values are so crucial.

There are several foundational principles that underlie the strategies and tactics that I want to describe in this chapter. The first is that three key concepts relating to structure must always be kept together in the structure and cannot be separated. Those concepts are authority, responsibility, and accountability. Any individual who is given a specific responsibility must be given adequate authority to accomplish the task. That individual must then be held accountable to ascertain that the responsibility has been fulfilled. Separating authority from responsibility creates frustration, and if accountability is absent, often creates ineffectiveness. Giving someone both authority and responsibility without demanding accountability is both dangerous and foolishness. All effective structures enable individuals to know clearly what their responsibilities are, provides them with more than adequate authority to carry out the responsibilities, and then demands that this individual provide measurable expectations of what will happen when the responsibilities are fulfilled (accountability).

The second foundational principle is that leaders must be given the freedom to lead. God expects those who are given gifts, talents, skills, and a call to lead with excellence. This means that leaders must be given broad authority to take strong leadership roles over areas for which they are responsible. Those same leaders should also expect to provide specific, measurable, behavioral, and tangible goals relating to outcomes and then be held accountable for those goals. However, in the pursuit of these goals leaders should be given wide latitude, flexibility, and protection by those to whom the leader is accountable. Leaders also need the freedom to fail so they will be willing to risk. Obviously, too much failure indicates a lack of wisdom and leadership. On the other hand, without risk and failure the organization is doomed to eventual decline and death.

The third foundational principle is that it is impossible to hold groups of people accountable, unless you are willing to dismiss the entire group when expectations are not met. I believe one of the main reasons that ecclesiastical bodies like committees and commissions is that these groups are ways for people to have influence without being held accountable, because we are usually unwilling to tell a group that it can no longer exist.

In most religious settings we find it almost impossible to confront an individual in order to tell that person he or she is performing poorly in conducting ministry. It is even more difficult to confront a group and inform the people in the group that they have failed to conduct ministry well. The group will not accept responsibility for such ineptness. Rather, individuals in the group will either become defensive and deny the accusation, or point fingers of blame at those within the group they perceived performed poorly. In the meantime nothing is accomplished. Almost every congregation has stories of how certain maintenance procedures have sat idle for months or years because a group of people could not settle on costs, purchases, or action.

Much of the literature on church leadership widely advises replacing committees with ministry teams. However, if teams are not held accountable for effective ministry, understanding that the entire team must be replaced if responsibilities are not met, than teams are simply committees that have been renamed.

The marriage of authority, responsibility, and accountability is best done with individuals, not groups. First, give an individual the authority and responsibility for a task. Then establish how this individual will be held accountable for results. Then let that individual select whomever she or he desires to help them. This person, however, clearly understands that he or she will be held accountable, not the people selected to minister with them. The second way is to make clear to a ministry team or even a committee that the leader of the team is going to be held accountable. If the team or committee fails to meet expectations, then the leader will be replaced for failing to lead well.

Adapting the John Carver Model of Governance

The new strategy we have employed in our region to implement these foundational principles is John Carver's model for board governance. The model is explained in Carver's book, *Boards That*

Make a Difference (Jossey-Bass, 1997). Although we like the essence of what Carver states, our region's board adapted his model for several reasons. The first reason relates to our understanding of leadership. We believe that individuals, not groups including boards, lead. Our perception of the Carver model, as presented, is that he places too much responsibility on the board for leading the organization. He has the CEO (Executive Minister, Pastor) leading the implementation of board policy. However, this person does not take a leading role in the creation of policy along with the board. Too much responsibility is placed upon the Chairman of the Board, who, from our perspective, is often not involved enough in the current affairs of the organization to take that role.

The second reason we adapted Carver was that we thought his four types of policy created more bureaucracy than was needed. Therefore we collapsed his last two areas of policy, relating to holding the CEO accountable and the board's internal processes, into one set of policies. The result is that our board deals with three sets of policies rather than four. However, beyond these two key changes we have taken the essence of Carver and implemented his teachings into the way our region's board now functions.

A key regional staff member led our board through this transition. This staff member began to study Carver soon after his initial work was published, and wrestled with how Carver's teaching related to congregations and other Christian organizations.

The first set of policies is called missional policies. Five such missional policies have been established by the board. The five missional policies listed in priority order are:

CHURCH REPRODUCTION—Planting healthy, reproducing churches among every group will be a top priority.

LEADERSHIP DEVELOPMENT—Developing effective church leadership will be a top priority of the region.

CHURCH TRAINING—Providing training for the purpose of growing healthy churches will be a top priority of the region.

GLOBAL MINISTRIES—A second-level priority of the region will be networking congregations and resources to grow healthy churches beyond the cultural and geographic boundaries of the region.

STATEGIC PARTNERSHIPS—A third level priority of the region will be working with other evangelical ministries, regardless of denomination, to grow healthy churches through alliances and projects that create a win for each ministry and for the advancement of God's Kingdom.

Our board determined that these five were crucial to the implementation of our mission. These policies are directed toward me, as the Executive Minister, and are designed to develop the areas for which I will be held accountable as the leader. My responsibility is to establish specific annual goals in each of the five areas, detailing how we will accomplish these missional objectives. At the end of the year I then provide an accounting for how well we performed during the year in achieving these five missional policies. There are limitations placed upon me in how I function as the Executive Minister. These are articulated in the next set of policies I will describe shortly.

The staff members of the region work for me, not the board. It is my responsibility to employ, oversee, and, as needed, remove staff members. Staff members do not interact with the board of the region in any official capacity. They do not come to board meetings unless invited. Therefore my task as the Executive Minister is to lead staff members to develop goals that will enable me, as the leader, to reach our five missional objectives. The logic is that if staff members accomplish their goals, then I reach my goals, and the board then is provided with a successful accounting at the end of the year of how we are implementing our mission. This is a major way our staff functions as a team.

The second set of policies is called boundary policies. These policies again are directed toward the Executive Minister. These are the policies that limit the Executive Minister by stating what I cannot do without special board approval. These policies govern my behavior as I implement the missional policies and lead the ministries of the region.

Therefore, all of these policies are written in the negative. The policies set boundaries. I am allowed to perform within these boundaries without seeking anyone's approval or permission; however, I am not allowed to go outside the boundaries. Should I go outside the boundaries and act in ways that have been proscribed as inappropriate, the board then holds me accountable for disobeying its policies. For example, I am responsible for creating and overseeing the region's budget. However, the creation of the budget and its oversight must be done within specific fiscal boundaries. If I exceed these boundaries in creating and administering the budget I will be held accountable. The board has created seven boundary policies that limit my conduct. In listing these policies it is important to realize that under most of the seven broad policies there are a number of more limiting policies that provide even smaller boundaries restricting the function of the Executive Minister. For example, even though I can create the region's budget, I must do it in relation to clearly stated board policies.

BIBLICAL AND MORAL INTEGRITY—The executive minister shall not fail to uphold high standards of biblical teaching and morality.

FINANCIAL PLANNING AND BUDGETING—Financial planning for any fiscal year or the remaining part of any fiscal year shall not deviate materially from the board's Mission Principles or risk financial jeopardy.

FINANCIAL CONDITION AND ACTIVITIES—The executive minister shall not allow the development of fiscal jeopardy or a material deviation of actual expenditures from board priorities established in Mission Principles.

ASSET PROTECTION—The executive minister shall not allow the assets to be unprotected, inadequately maintained, or necessarily risked.

COMPENSATION AND BENEFITS—The executive minister shall not cause or allow jeopardy to fiscal integrity or public image.

TREATMENT OF STAFF—The executive minister may not cause or allow conditions that are unfair or illegal.

COMMUNICATION WITH AND SUPPORT TO THE BOARD—The executive minister shall not permit the board to be uninformed or unsupported in its work.

Carver states that each policy is written in the broadest form possible. Then under each broad statement other policies are written that begin to narrow down what the leader cannot do.

The third set of policies is called accountability policies. These policies are directed toward the chairperson of the board. The person who holds this position is also the President of the region. These policies as implemented by the board chairperson are designed to make certain that the leader of the region, the Executive Minister, fulfills the mission policies and avoids violating the boundary policies. There are three major accountability policies. These policies are as follows:

STEWARDSHIP TO CHRIST FOR THOSE HE CALLS US TO SERVE—The board shall maintain an active connection to the "moral ownership" of the region: Christ and the churches he has called this region to serve.

MAINTAINING THE PROCESS OF THE BOARD—The board shall conduct itself with discipline and integrity with regard to its own process of governance.

MONITORING THE PERFORMANCE OF THE EXECUTIVE MINISTER—The board's sole official connection to the operating organization of the region, its achievement, and conduct shall be through the executive minister.

Again, as with the boundary policies, there are more detailed and limiting policies articulated under each of these three broad policy statements.

This governance model allows the board to spend the majority of its board meeting time focusing on two crucial areas. The first area is board training. We conduct training in such areas as leadership development, understanding the current culture and its impact on the environment for ministry, congregational reproduction and development, financial development, and discerning the impact of the future on ministry concerns.

Our board meetings, of which there are four a year, normally last four hours, including a time to eat a meal together. The first hour is dedicated to training. The Executive Minister is responsible to either conduct the training or bring in a qualified person to lead the training. The rest of the meeting is dedicated to prayer, business, discussing the future, and eating.

The second area on which our board now has time to focus is the future. The Executive Minster is given the responsibility of conducting current ministry within the prescribed boundaries. Therefore, current business, for the most part, does require board attention.

At the beginning of the year we create an annual agenda. This agenda is designed to create a period of discussion in each board meeting about decisions we need to make relating to the future. Little time needs to be spent in board meetings focusing on current issues. It is more important that we project into the future and discuss those issues that will shape the region's ministry during the next five to ten years.

A Strategy for Changing Structure

Prior to suspending our by-laws, the Executive Minister was given much latitude in leading. However, this was not due to an intentional structure. This person had held the position of Executive Minister for twenty-five years and therefore possessed a great amount of influence due to his strong leadership over the years. He was also recognized in ABC circles as being an effective executive and carried significant influence nationally. This recognition pleased many influential people in the region since it increased their status and that of the region with national leaders. It also enabled the Executive Minister to leverage his experience into new endeavors of leadership that enabled him to keep growing and learning.

The region under his leadership had become a well-run bureaucracy. In the early years of his tenure the region had experienced significant growth. This growth enabled him to expand his staff and programs. This bureaucracy also enabled him, as the one consistent leader over other positions that were constantly changing, to gain influence because of his knowledge and expertise in how ministry was to be conducted. In many ways he had the influence that a long-tenured, successful pastor carries with a congregation that has seen a great deal of success. His leadership enabled many in the region to be proud of what had been established.

The changing needs required for effective twenty-first century ministry demanded a new kind of leadership. The region needed a leader who would come in and bring renewal both to the region and to congregations. The current structure, while excellent at maintaining the status quo, would not allow a change agent leader to produce renewal. This was particularly true if those with vested interests in the current structure did not want to pursue the kind of change that was necessary. The current structure at that time gave these individuals the power to stop any systemic change even if that change produced more effective ministry.

The region had hired a new Executive Minister who was both a leader and a change agent. He would lead the region to develop a new mission and embrace a new structure. His strategies for implementing the mission and changing structure would never have come about if it were not for his leadership. Leaders and leadership always precede changes in mission and structure. Without leadership there is no systemic change to any organization. After all no one deliberately goes through the pain of changing his or her own skeleton. Instead, we all find ways to cope with current ineptness creating more dysfunction in the process.

One thing we who were new to the region had learned in former ministries was that even good changes are resisted by those who hold current positions of influence, if that change means they no longer have influence. We had also learned that most who were in positions of influence now would resist change, again, no matter how effective that change might be, since those changes would be perceived as a repudiation of their current leadership, which in most cases was true.

Therefore, we knew we had to do something about structure if our new mission, vision, and values were going to be adopted. We believed in strong leadership, which meant that once the mission was adopted and once the vision was cast the leader needed to be given the freedom to lead. This meant the leader could not be second-guessed all the time for what she or he was doing to bring a change that would implement the mission and achieve the vision. It meant the leader could not be encumbered with bureaucratic restrictions that either inhibited what needed to be accomplished or slowed it down as it was going through channels. The leader did need to be held accountable, but that accountability needed to be one that related to the accomplishment of goals and results, not the process by which these goals and results were achieved.

As Baptists we were used to structures that usually required voting and approval before any major decisions could be implemented. Also, we were used to boards and groups that upon hearing of leadership decisions that bothered people, presumed to have the right to bring the leader to account for causing people to feel discomfort. I have often told pastors and board members alike that most lay board members would never put up with any form of employment that was structured like the pastor's job. Where else does a person with any degree of education work all month making decisions only to have a group of people come together who know very little about that position and the demands related to it and then evaluate all that person has done? Every layperson in the world wants a job where she or he has enough respect from his or her employer to make most job-related decisions without being second-guessed on a weekly or monthly basis. Such a structure is bad enough if the pastor or region's leader is maintaining the status quo. However, when renewal is at stake, which means that people will become upset with required changes, this kind of structure is damning.

Theological Assumptions

There are a number of theological assumptions behind the decisions we have made as a region. These assumptions inform our beliefs and in turn our behaviors. These assumptions have caused us to not only seek renewal but hold firm to what we believe that renewal should entail. The following articulates the most basic assumptions that have led to the region functioning as it does today.

The Mission: As stated previously we believe that the mission of the region is the correct one. Our goal of helping congregations fulfill the Great Commission is based upon theological assumptions we hold as leaders.

The God of the Bible is a missionary God. Since the fall of the human race God seeks to bring people back to God. God blessed Abraham and his descendents so that the world through them would be blessed. God expected Israel to be a light to the Gentiles and condemned the nation when it failed in this mission (Isa. 49:6; Rom. 10:18-21). Therefore God provided redemption for the world through the Lord Jesus Christ. Jesus Christ while on earth stated that he would build his church and that the gates of hell would not prove to be stronger than it. The Apostle Paul next taught that God displayed his wisdom by bringing both Jews and Gentiles together as they both exercised faith in Jesus Christ to become part of this new entity called the church. The Book of Revelation then reveals that at the end of time women and men from all across history and the world who exercised faith in Jesus Christ will stand with him as part of his redeemed people, called the church.

In light of this very brief summary of God's revelation, we believe that the Church has one mission. That mission is to be God's missionary entity in this world to call women and men to repentance through faith in Jesus Christ. We believe that God created the church primarily as a missional entity. Each local congregation is to be involved in carrying out this mission as its primary responsibility, above all others. The goal of our region then has been to assist congregations in becoming missional entities. The region has become a missional entity, but the region's mission is not the same as the congregation's. Our mission is to mobilize, assist, motivate, and encourage congregations in the accomplishment of the mission God has given to them.

One of the most challenging tasks we have had as a region is to help congregations understand that they were not created to take care of their needs first. As missional agencies congregations exist primarily for the people who are yet to join them in their mission. Existing congregations are to serve those who may currently see them as irrelevant or foolish. When congregations begin to understand that they exist for others it causes them to focus outward and that is what begins to bring health and growth.

The Image of Jesus Christ: Leaders understand that metaphors and images determine what people believe and how they act. The only physical description we are given of Jesus Christ in the Bible is found in Revelation 1:12-16. This image reflects the Savior of the world who has had His glory returned to him. The resurrected and glorified Lord stands before the Apostle John as the judge and leader of his church. He judges congregations that fail to carry out his mission. However, he leads his church from a position of power and glory.

It is this image we have wanted to convey to pastors and congregations. Prior to the turnaround the image of Jesus Christ that permeated the region was one of a suffering savior and a kindly friend. Both of these images are biblical and convey great significance. However, neither one of those images was creating within congregations a sense of effectiveness in ministry, hope of changed communities, and an abundance of new disciples willing to follow a savior who had provided for their redemption. Our goal was to add other biblical metaphors to the thinking of leaders. We helped them understand that a shepherd had roles that often were not communicated in our religious romanticism. So too, is the image of the Lord of the church. Because of his resurrection, ascension, and glorification Jesus expects the church, in dependence upon him, to accomplish great things.

Congregations and pastors honor the practices of chaplains—smallness is beneficial and family as the norm—because they have an incomplete image of the Lord of the church. This incomplete image comes because our metaphors of who Jesus Christ are often insufficient or understated. Jesus is a successful leader, calling his church to grow and accomplish great things in mission.

A Sense of Urgency: Any congregation must ask, What difference does faith in Jesus Christ make eternally? If the answer to that question is, "the answer is unclear," then it seems to me there is no sense of urgency about communicating the Gospel message. If on the other hand faith in Jesus Christ determines eternal destinies, than urgency becomes a major issue for pastors, congregations, and denominations.

Until recently, most of the congregations in our region acted as though there was no sense of urgency about communicating the Gospel message. Most congregations focused on their own needs. Any concern for "lost" people was for the most part handled by sending mission dollars to denominational missions programs so others in distant places could fulfill the responsibility of communicating the Gospel message. Yet the majority of people in our congregations believed that one's informed faith in Jesus Christ did make an eternal difference. However, congregations acted as though it really did not matter to the lost people surrounding them, that these people would die without any knowledge about who Jesus Christ was and what He could do for them. There simply was no sense of urgency.

Our theology as leaders demanded a sense of urgency . We believed that Jesus gave the Great Commission to his church because there is a sense of urgency. Believers will have all of eternity to worship God and Jesus Christ. Believers for eternity will be able to fellowship with their Lord and other Christians. We will have the eternal opportunity to sit at the feet of Jesus Christ and be taught. However, our God has only given us one lifetime to make disciples for Jesus Christ. Congregations that focus on worship, fellowship, and teaching often reflect groups that have lost a sense of urgency. In fact this is where our congregations were. They were fighting the worship wars or ignoring them completely. Our congregations were trying small groups for their own members. Our congregations were filled with people going to conferences and learning about Scripture through a variety of media. However, our congregational baptismals were used only rarely. Not only were attendance and mission dollars declining but so too were baptisms.

Therefore, we taught congregations that they needed a mission and a vision. We also taught them that all congregations really have the same mission. That mission is to make more disciples for Jesus Christ. Jesus gave the church this mission because he understood the urgency of reaching people before they pass from this world to the next. We worked at helping our congregations feel a sense of urgency about reaching people in their communities. Our congregations had to realize that we live in a pagan culture that is increasing in violence where many people need multiple contacts with believers before they will even be open to and be able to hear a clear presentation of the Gospel message. We wanted them to write vision statements in terms of changed communities. The assumption was that communities change as more and more people come to faith in Jesus and begin to live as a disciple of Jesus Christ.

These are the key theological assumptions that inform the beliefs of the Executive Minister and his staff, the region's board, and our mentoring pastors. The basis unit of mission, the congregation, is compelled by a sense of urgency to work diligently at making more disciples for Jesus Christ. God expects these units to be healthy, growing, and vital since their leader is the successful savior who leads them from the perspective of a resurrected, glorified Lord.

Mission Determines Polity

The problem with denominations is that they want to shape the mission around their polity, rather than shape the polity around the mission. The latter view is the spirit of all the founding fathers and mothers of every denomination, while the former is the sorry state of *every* denomination today. The lack of mission urgency in North America means that denominational leaders think they still have time to develop modest, incremental strategic plans to tinker with polity, and time afterwards to then go about mission. The truth is just the opposite. The eternal destinies of individuals do not allow such laxness.

First I come at polity from a negative perspective. As I look at the world we are trying to reach, with the missional urgency we embrace, all the major streams of denominational polities seem quite deficient. Structure either helps or inhibits mission while at the same time infecting and determining an organization's culture. I find that all polities inhibit mission and create a conspiracy of smallness that has come to be valued at the expense of effective ministry.

I find that current church polities assume a world that no longer exists. Current ecclesiastical polities reflect political models that worked with some degree of effectiveness in agrarian societies. The reality is that we now live in an informational society that is evolving from the industrial one. We in the West also live in cultures that are no longer Christian. They are pagan, and shared cultural Christian values no longer affect thought and action for most people, including Christians. Therefore people do not come to congregational life and behavior with a common background or understanding. They also come with very different values and expectations, many of which place a higher value on results than outdated processes.

All current polity systems perpetuate models of governance that lead to organizational hierarchies (some through position and others through tenure) and create bureaucracies. These models of organization are rejected in almost all organizations today except for the church. Almost every congregation I have ever consulted with has told me that their one problem, unique to congregations with their polity, is that they have too many committees. Congregations think that this issue, which is usually described in a polity context, is unique to them. They do not realize that their congregation is simply reflecting what their denomination and judicatories are already doing. Each congregation sees itself imprisoned by their structure and wish they had the structure of another polity when it comes to organization.

Our current polity systems usually enfranchise those people who are the least able to lead while tying the hands of the most creative and able leaders. This statement assumes that the most able leaders are still around after any brief exposure to how religious bodies function. Our polities allow the managers, administrators, and politicians who understand complex bureaucratic systems to become the leaders in congregational, judicatory, and denominational life. In the meantime these systems weed out those with entrepreneurial and leadership skills. These people for the most part leave and create their own ministries or shadow organizations that go around the bureaucracies created by our polities.

Our current polities create a theology of smallness, since that is all these polities will tolerate in a modern, complex, and fragmented world. There is great disdain for those congregations that are missional in organization, motivated by vision, and entrepreneurial in ministry. These are the congregations that in our day have become large and have the opportunity and ability to change communities. The criticism we often hear of such congregations is that they are a mile wide and an inch deep. Yet often those offering the criticisms are involved in congregations that are an inch wide and an inch deep. Our denominational polities have created organizations that promote a conspiracy of smallness that allows a handful of controllers to focus the church on membership privileges that are defined by their personal and family needs and desires.

I come now at polity from a positive perspective. I believe the reason that the New Testament does not provide instruction on the correct polity for congregations and in turn denominations (as indicated by the fact that all current polity systems pick and choose though passages that fit their system, while ignoring those that do not) is that our Jesus saw the church as a growing, living, breathing organism that would constantly be changing and morphing in relation to the culture. The polities of the fifteenth and sixteenth centuries do not work in the twenty-first century. If they did the Church of Jesus Christ in the Western world would be far more effective than it is. Therefore, I believe we need to look at flexible polities that fit the requirement of biblical principles about mission, rather than trying to prop up idealized structures that reflect agrarian life in past centuries.

First, we must get back to honoring leaders and placing a New Testament value on leadership. God has provided the church with people who posses this gift and people to whom God as given leadership skills and talents in abundance. We therefore need polities that let leaders lead with excellence.

Second, we must restore some kind of polity that marries authority, responsibility, and accountability. All current polities separate these three concepts. Some polities do it in theory while all do it in practice. Congregations are scared to death to put authority and responsibility together because most believe it will create organizational monsters with dictatorial leaders. This fear is well founded, if there is not clear and powerful accountability. Yet because of our concept of "family" we run from accountability like animals from a forest fire. So we create polities that separate authority from responsibility, resulting in frustration and the loss of our best leaders.

Third, we need polities that constantly push the congregation to be answerable to its mission and vision. Leaders should be training congregations to expect health and growth. Congregations should be upset when a year goes by if conversions and baptisms decrease. The church exists for others, and when others stop coming and cease experiencing eternal changes, congregations should start asking their leaders why they continue to meet, since their purpose for meeting is not being realized. The purpose of church is not just to meet and see a budget met.

Fourth, we need polities that allow the most gifted, committed, and involved lay leaders to understand that the epitome of service in congregational life is leading ministries that equip new disciples to make more disciples and train them to become leaders. The highest position is not sitting on a board and being in charge. Hopefully, good board members will take the Jimmy Carter approach to life and learn that true significance for the former president has come not from holding office but in serving people.

Finally, we must get away from the notion in congregational life that everyone has an equal say. Everyone has equal standing before God in Jesus Christ. However, the right to speak and influence congregational life and behavior should be granted in proportion to one's maturity as a disciple and ministry as a servant.

The whole point of polity is to enable the Church of Jesus Christ to practice the following:

- Produce radical disciples of Jesus Christ

- Create disciples who choose mission over membership

- Develop leaders who resist control

- Motivate congregations to practice unrelenting outreach

- Empower spiritual leaders to reproduce spiritual leaders

- Select leaders who will get out of the Spirit's way.

A FINAL PIECE OF THE STORY

I consulted with a small congregation in our region that had seen another pastor, in a line of several before him, leave in discouragement. The congregation had declined in average attendance from 117 to ninety. Upon leaving the church building at the end of the consultation I told a colleague that this church will never go anywhere if some people do not leave. Three emotional terrorists controlled the system and were not going to give up power.

However, the congregation at our suggestion invited an intentional interim to be their pastor while we helped them locate a new leader. The interim within three months through fairly bold actions took power from the controllers and as a result they left the congregation. Once that occurred the congregation began to grow. This growth during the interim period attracted a young growth pastor from another American Baptist region to the congregation.

Under his leadership a number of changes, begun during the interim's tenure, came to fulfillment. The congregation became outwardly focused in mission and began to take seriously the belief that it exists to reach the community. The structure changed with the elimination of the then current board and all committees. The congregation is now led by a pastor and teams where passions and gifts are matched with ministries. There is an emphasis on prayer, excellence in worship, and preaching that reflects God's heart for a lost world. Ultimately all ministries and service are evaluated in relation to the congregation's mission.

God has blessed the actions of the pastor and the congregation. In three years 259 new members had joined. Over one-half of them have come by way of conversion. The worship attendance is averaging 550 and on certain Sundays is over 600. This congregation and pastor are a testimony to all the congregations in the region that God's primary unit of mission is the local congregation.

Only God grows the Church. However I am convinced that God has blessed our region. The reason is we have hit the Bull's eye in focusing on healthy growing congregations that are committed to fulfilling God's great commission to the Church.